D0445275

Gordon, Philip H.,
1962-
  Winning the right
war

WINNING THE RIGHT WAR

WINNING THE RIGHT WAR

The Path to Security for
America and the World

PHILIP H. GORDON

TIMES BOOKS

HENRY HOLT AND COMPANY   NEW YORK

Times Books
Henry Holt and Company, LLC
Publishers since 1866
175 Fifth Avenue
New York, New York 10010
www.henryholt.com

Henry Holt® is a registered trademark of
Henry Holt and Company, LLC.

Library of Congress Cataloging-in-Publication Data
Gordon, Philip H., date.
  Winning the right war : the path to security for America and the world / Philip H.
Gordon.—1st. ed.
      p. cm.
  Includes bibliographical references and index.
  ISBN-13: 978-0-8050-8657-7
  ISBN-10: 0-8050-8657-9
  1. United States—Foreign relations—2001–   2. National security—United States.
3. War on Terrorism, 2001–   4. United States—Foreign relations—Middle East.
5. Middle East—Foreign relations—United States.   6. World politics—1989–
7. United States—Foreign relations—Philosophy.   8. Cold War.   9. United
States—Foreign relations—1945–1989.   10. World politics—1945–1989.
I. Title.
  E895.G67 2007
  327.7305609'051—dc22   2007019032

Henry Holt books are available for special promotions and premiums.
For details contact: Director, Special Markets.

First Edition 2007

Designed by Kelly Too

Printed in the United States of America
10   9   8   7   6   5   4   3   2   1

To Rachel, Noah, Ben, and "Deeds"

★ ★ ★

★ ★ ★ Contents

★ ★ ★ Introduction

Six years after the start of the "war on terror," Americans are less safe, our enemies are stronger and more numerous, and the war's key geographic battleground—the Middle East—is dangerously unstable. In Iraq, thousands of American soldiers, and tens of thousands of Iraqi soldiers and civilians, have been killed or wounded while more than 150,000 U.S. troops fight to contain an insurgency and a civil war—at a cost of over $300 million per day. In Iran, an Islamic fundamentalist regime remains firmly in power and is defiantly pursuing a nuclear weapons program, undermining American efforts in Iraq, and subsidizing increasingly brazen terrorist groups in the Middle East. Palestine is now led by one terrorist group, Hamas, while another, Hezbollah, is increasingly popular and influential in Lebanon, having proclaimed victory in its war with Israel in the summer of 2006. Syria remains under an anti-American dictatorship allied to Iran, and no peace process between Israel and any of its neighbors exists. More broadly, according to repeated public opinion polls, the popularity and credibility of the United States is at an all-time low—Hezbollah leader Sheikh

Hassan Nasrallah is far more popular in the Muslim world than President Bush; most Muslims would prefer to see China or France replace America as the dominant outside power; and majorities even among America's traditional allies now have a highly unfavorable view of the United States. While the U.S. homeland has not been attacked successfully since 9/11, Osama bin Laden remains at large, and there have been numerous major terrorist attacks all around the globe in that six-year period—approximately twice as many as in the six years before the war on terror was launched. Far from being "on the march," democracy in the Middle East is in trouble, and where it has advanced in most cases—including Palestine, Iraq, Egypt, and Lebanon—it has produced unintended and often unwanted consequences. For a war that has now been going on longer than World War II, the balance sheet is dismal.

The Bush administration always warned that overcoming the terrorist threat would take time. One possible conclusion, therefore, is that the challenge posed by Islamist terrorism is so enormous that the current difficulties are to be expected, and that there is in any case no alternative to the administration's approach. According to the journalist and author Max Boot, a prominent supporter of George W. Bush's foreign policy, "It is far too soon to judge the results of the President's grand strategy of transforming the Middle East, which is still in its early stages."[1] This is the argument used by the White House when it claims "significant progress" in the war on terror, makes the case for resolve and perseverance, and warns its critics that they risk encouraging the terrorists by raising questions about the administration's approach.[2]

An alternative explanation of the failure to make more progress could be that the United States is mostly on the right track but simply failing to put sufficient resources and energy into the war effort. This is the argument made by many of President Bush's critics on the right, such as former Speaker of the House Newt Gingrich, who argues that Bush's "strategies are not wrong, but they are failing." Gingrich believes the struggle between the West and the forces of militant Islam should be considered an "emerging World War III" and argues that it can be won by mobilizing more "energy, resources, and intensity."[3]

It would be comforting to believe that the main cause of America's difficulties has been the lack of time or resources. But few signs indicate that things are moving in the right direction, and there is little reason to believe that "staying the course"—or indeed expanding the fight—will succeed. In its first six years, the Bush administration's war on terror has cost hundreds of billions of dollars, exhausted the U.S. military, alienated friends and allies, and squandered America's moral authority, yet has made little progress toward its ultimate goals.

Sadly, there is a more compelling conclusion. The administration is failing because it is fighting the wrong war. It is fighting against an alleged single enemy, when the enemy is extremely diverse. It is putting its faith in tough talk and military power, when ideology, intelligence, diplomacy, and defense are in fact more important. It is polarizing the public and alienating the world when national unity and international legitimacy are badly needed. It is focusing on a tactic, terrorism, when the real issue is how to address the political, diplomatic, social, and economic factors that lead people to use that tactic. And it is assuming there is a set number of terrorist enemies who must be stopped or killed, when in fact the number of potential terrorists varies greatly, in part as a function of U.S. policy itself. Put most simply, the administration is fighting the "war on terror" like a traditional, hot war—taking the offensive militarily, aiming to destroy a fixed enemy, expanding executive authority, and downplaying the importance of legitimacy—when something more akin to the Cold War—a long, patient, moral struggle against a hostile ideology—is required. Until America's leaders learn to think differently about the new war, they will continue to lose it.

From the moment George W. Bush started talking about a "war on terror"—less than twelve hours after the 9/11 attacks—critics have argued that the president's terminology was flawed. Declaring war might well have been useful to rally public opinion, but it had the significant disadvantage of implying there was a military solution to the problem, and it endowed the terrorists with a warrior status they did not deserve. The object of the war was also a problem— terrorism was merely a method, not an organization or country, and it covered such a broad range of activities that it risked confusing Americans about just whom they were at war against.[4]

These were sound critiques, but over time they have become moot. The "war on terror" has now entered the public vernacular and is used by both the administration and its critics to refer to the set of policies designed to protect America and its allies from the threat of terrorism from Islamist extremists. Moreover, and more important, the debate about the name tends to obscure the fact that the real problem is not so much what we call the Bush administration's approach to terrorism but the flawed assumptions and principles on which it is based. The "war on crime," the "war on drugs," and the "war on poverty" are also highly flawed concepts (as are all such simplifications), but we judge—and we should judge—those endeavors by the sets of policies that they encompass rather than by their names. A more accurate description of the target for this war—al Qaeda, its affiliates, imitators, and sponsors—would doubtless have made more sense. But a war on terror it was and a war on terror it will likely remain. In this book I want to focus on the best ways to deal with this serious challenge rather than to perpetuate a largely meaningless semantic debate.

It is not too late to start fighting the right war, but doing so will require major changes in U.S. policy. Like the Bush approach, a new strategy for fighting terrorism will seek victory, but it will recognize that victory is more likely to be achieved by maintaining America's strength, cohesion, and appeal than by destroying its enemies through the force of arms. The right war will require continued military operations. But it will also require efforts to improve America's moral standing in the world, which has been deeply damaged by the war in Iraq and by U.S. policy on detainees at Guantánamo and elsewhere. It will require resisting the temptation to hype the terrorist threat for political purposes and a realization that militaristic reactions to terrorism can play into the terrorists' hands and potentially do more harm than good. It will require understanding that democracy promotion in the Middle East will not quickly or necessarily lead to peace, but that good governance, education, and economic modernization can help alleviate the feelings of frustration and humiliation that fuel terrorism. The right war will require a dramatic reduction in America's dependence on imported oil, which in turn will not only reduce available funding to those who support terrorism but also promote democracy in the Middle East by removing the oil lifeline that allows regimes in that region to avoid giving their people a voice. It will require restoring America's reputation as an honest broker in a much more active quest for Israeli-Arab peace, the absence of which is a far greater stimulation of global terrorism than the Bush administration and its supporters like to admit. The right war will require seeking a sustainable peace in Iraq, containment of Iran, a far greater commitment to the people and government of Afghanistan, greater use of leverage and engagement with Pakistan, and new efforts to repair the strained relations with Turkey, the most advanced democracy in the Muslim world. And the right war will require a new form of diplomacy to ensure the global legitimacy and support of allies, without which no war on terror can be won.

This alternative path will not be easy. Each time a new terrorist attack occurs—or even each time a new threat is revealed—there will be a temptation to go on the offensive, rounding up and holding suspects or deploying American military power. Politically, it is difficult for American leaders to argue for patience and restraint, especially if their opponents are offering "moral clarity" and promising quick fixes based on America's unmatched brute power. It is difficult for leaders to put the terrorist threat into perspective when hyping the threat has political advantages. But the yardstick for judging the war on terror should not be how tough it sounds but how effective it is, and that requires a fundamental change of approach.

The precedent of America's triumph in the Cold War should give us confidence that patience, strength, resolve, and good sense can once again lead us to victory. The new challenge is not identical to the Cold War, of course, but their similarities—as long-term struggles against insidious and violent ideologies—suggest that there is much to learn from this recent, and successful, experience. As in the Cold War, we must be willing to fight to defend ourselves and our interests, but we must also recognize that the war will be won only when our enemy's ideology is defeated and our adversaries abandon it. Just as the Cold War was not won or lost in Vietnam, the war on terror will not be won or lost in Iraq. The decisive terrain for this struggle is in the hearts, minds, and souls of a billion individuals across the greater Middle East, South and Southeast Asia, and Western Europe—not on the streets of Baghdad.

It is difficult today to imagine a world without the Islamist terrorist threat—just as it was difficult for the last generations to imagine a world without the communist threat. But the extremist ideology responsible for the current threat is doomed to fail just like the extremist ideology that preceded it. Terrorism will not go away entirely, any more than other types of violent crime that have been around for centuries. But its sources can be dried up, its access to the most dangerous weapons curtailed, and its political motivations significantly reduced. With confidence in our values and our way of life—and a determination to preserve all that is good about both—we can defeat the scourge of our time as our predecessors defeated the scourge of theirs.

This book presents a new strategy for confronting the terrorist challenge. It is not meant to be a comprehensive policy agenda but rather a plea for a new philosophy to guide the way we think about, and act against, the terrorist threat. The current approach is not working, nor is it likely to work, because it is based on a flawed understanding of the nature of the challenge and a counterproductive strategy for dealing with it. As Americans look beyond the presidency of George W. Bush, they must seize the opportunity to rethink the current approach and consider alternative paths to security for America and the world. The stakes could not be higher.

WINNING THE RIGHT WAR

1 ★ THE WRONG WAR

It was probably not the president's all-time favorite holiday break. Indeed, as 2007 began, George W. Bush was at his ranch in Crawford, Texas, as usual, but he was not watching college football or clearing brush. Instead he was huddled with his political and foreign policy advisers, preparing for what many were saying would be "the most important speech of his presidency."[1] They all knew what was at stake—not just Bush's presidency but the security of the United States and the lives of its fine young soldiers. The speech had been delayed for a month as the administration examined policy options and debated what message to send in outlining a "new strategy" for the war in Iraq. The president and his team understood that with only two years left in his term, this speech to the nation would perhaps be a final opportunity to win back the American public's waning support for a war that was widely perceived to be failing.

The previous weeks and months had not gone well for Bush. In November, the Democrats took back the majority in both houses of Congress, in an election that many read as a repudiation of the president's foreign policy. In the wake of the election, with his overall job approval rating at 34 percent and with public support for his Iraq policy at an all-time low of 31 percent, Bush felt obliged to fire his long-standing secretary of defense, Donald Rumsfeld, whom he had publicly promised to retain only weeks before. In Iraq itself, the insurgency that many had predicted would die down was instead raging, and the country appeared to be sliding toward civil war. December 2006 turned out to be one of the deadliest months since the start of the war, bringing the total number of American military fatalities to more than 3,000 and the tally of U.S. wounded to more than 20,000. Iraqi civilian fatalities were estimated to be more than 30,000 for the year 2006 alone.[2]

Also in December 2006, the Iraq Study Group—a bipartisan group of eminent Americans under the leadership of former secretary of state James Baker and former congressman Lee Hamilton—issued its long-awaited report on Iraq, which turned out to be a stinging rebuke of the Bush administration's policies and a call for a dramatically revised approach. The report described the situation in Iraq as "grave and deteriorating," in great contrast to the "progress" the administration had been claiming for more than three years, and it also called for a major course correction, notably via a drawdown of American combat forces by the start of 2008. More broadly, the report encouraged the administration to embark on a "diplomatic offensive" in the Middle East by actively relaunching diplomatic efforts to promote peace between Israelis and Palestinians and opening up a dialogue with adversaries like Syria and Iran.[3]

In its bipartisan makeup and connections to the presidency of Bush's father, whom Baker had served as secretary of state, the Iraq Study Group offered more than just policy guidance on Iraq; it offered the president "political cover" for a potential change of course. Already, Bush's second term was widely perceived to be of a significantly different character than his first. Some of the most prominent "neo-conservative" architects of the Iraq war had left the administration, and Secretary of State Condoleezza Rice was emphasizing diplomacy and multilateralism. Bush himself had signaled a new desire to repair America's frayed ties with its traditional European allies, and he even reversed himself by endorsing the European nuclear diplomacy with Iran. And now the controversial Rumsfeld had been replaced by Robert Gates, a pragmatic "realist" from the George H. W. Bush administration who had himself been a member of the Iraq Study Group. Gates's quick and overwhelming confirmation by the Senate reinforced the sense in Washington that a new approach was in the offing—not only for Iraq but also for U.S. foreign policy and the war on terror more broadly.[4]

But that's not what happened. Instead, in his prime-time speech from the White House library on January 10, 2007, Bush took less than twenty minutes to make clear that he was sticking to his guns. Far from changing America's foreign policy course, he recommitted himself and his presidency to it. He would not withdraw troops from Iraq but instead would send 20,000 more of them. He would not distinguish between the war in Iraq and the war on terror but would continue to speak of them as one and the same—as the "decisive ideological struggle of our time." He would not embrace a bipartisan approach to Iraq designed to bolster domestic support but would continue down a path opposed by clear majorities in Congress and among the public at large. He would not launch a diplomatic offensive in the Middle East or adopt other new measures to win greater global legitimacy but would continue with an approach that was almost certain to garner little international support.[5] In short, as the conservative columnist Gerard Baker put it, the president's speech was not the announcement of a new direction but a "clarion reaffirmation . . . of the entire foreign policy strategy that drove the Bush administration in the weeks and months after September 11, 2001. It was a defiant and ringing rededication of a beleaguered president in the final two years of his term to the revolution in global affairs he unleashed five years ago."[6]

In recommitting to his course of action in Iraq and in continuing to insist that Iraq was the "central front in the war on terror," Bush was doing more than demonstrating his famous resolve. He was also perpetuating a conception of the fight against terrorism that has been fundamentally flawed from the start. His determination to fight and win a war was perhaps admirable. Unfortunately, he was still determined to fight the wrong war.

A FLAWED DIAGNOSIS

Perhaps the most important step in meeting the terrorist challenge is to understand the nature, sources, and causes of the threat. This is no easy task, but it has been made even more difficult by President Bush's tendency to mischaracterize them. Bush has given many different explanations of terrorism over the years, but the main ones seem to be a hatred for freedom, the lack of democracy, and America's past unwillingness to respond forcefully enough to terrorist acts. The picture painted is thus one of some fixed set of "evil-doers," driven to violence by the absence of democracy in their homelands, who attack America and its allies because they hate our freedoms and because we are perceived to be weak. As a basis for understanding—and therefore dealing with—the terrorist threat, this explanation is exceedingly partial and misleading.

Bush regularly suggests that terrorists attack the United States and its allies because they hate the freedoms we enjoy. Just nine days after the 9/11 attacks, he declared that the terrorists hate "our freedom of religion, our freedom of speech, our freedom to vote and assemble and disagree with each other."[7] They are "at war against us," he continued to argue more than five years later, "because they hate everything America stands for—and we stand for freedom. . . . They can't stand the thought that people can go into the public square in America and express their differences with government. They can't stand the thought that the people get to decide the future of our country by voting."[8]

The idea that terrorists attack because they hate freedom, however, is misguided. The explanation is convenient, because it suggests that there is nothing we can do about it (since they hate "who we are" rather than "what we do"), and it is harmful because it suggests that the only way to defeat such terrorists is to kill or capture them all, since we're obviously not prepared to sacrifice our freedom to appease them. But there is little evidence to suggest that hatred of freedom is in fact a primary cause of terrorism, and much to suggest that it is not.

At the most superficial level, if freedom were the main

target for terrorists, they would be just as likely to attack Switzerland, Canada, Costa Rica, or Sweden as to attack the United States, which is clearly not the case. Indeed, Saudi Arabia, Pakistan, and Egypt have been much more frequent targets of jihadist attacks than the United States, and it is surely not because the terrorists hate the individual liberties and elected governments in those countries.

Extensive polling in the Muslim world also challenges the notion of a significant link between terrorism and a hatred for freedom. While many Islamist ideologues often do express revulsion with the personal liberties and sexual freedom enjoyed in Western countries, it turns out that even most of the Muslims who support terrorism and trust Osama bin Laden favor elected government, personal liberty, educational opportunity, and economic choice.[9] The Palestinian pollster Khalil Shikaki finds the same pattern among Palestinians, a majority of whom admire U.S.—and even Israeli— political culture, even as many of them support terrorism against Israel.[10] Some Muslim extremists may not like American-style democracy, but that is not why they become terrorists and not why others support them.

Bush's link between authoritarianism and terrorism is more accurate, because living in repressive societies probably does contribute to the frustration that helps drive people to commit violent acts. But as a central explanation for the contemporary terrorist phenomenon it is inadequate, and as the primary guideline for policymaking it is counterproductive and even dangerous.

First and most obviously, plenty of nondemocratic and even repressive societies have long existed without having produced any terrorism at all. It is thus hard to explain why the absence of democracy in the Muslim world would be the main explanation for Islamist terrorism, when the democracy variable does not seem to have that effect elsewhere—in China, Zimbabwe, North Korea, or Cuba, for example.

Moreover, as political scientist Gregory Gause has pointed out, most recent terrorist attacks have actually occurred in democracies and both the victims and perpetrators are often citizens of democracies.[11] Of the thousands of terrorist incidents that have taken place since 2000, the vast majority have been in countries categorized as "free" or "partially free."[12] The recent terrorist attacks in countries like Britain, Spain, and India—perpetrated by people who live there—cannot be explained by any lack of democracy in those countries.

The focus on the lack of democracy as a key cause of the terrorism problem also risks implying that promoting elections in the countries many terrorists come from is a promising path to security. At least in the short term, however, holding free elections before the social and institutional conditions for democracy are in place would almost certainly create new problems. In recent democratic elections in Palestine, Iraq, and Egypt, the winners were the Palestinian terrorist group Hamas, Iraqi Islamist parties, and Egypt's Muslim Brotherhood, not exactly the freedom-loving groups the Bush administration had in mind as an antidote to terrorism. Allowing these groups to come to power and then fail may well be necessary as a means of defeating their ideology, but the damage they can do in the meantime needs to be acknowledged. Iraq is now free from the grip of the horrible dictatorship of Saddam Hussein. But while today's Iraq is certainly more "democratic" than it was under

Saddam—a good thing for many Iraqis—it is also a far greater source of terrorism now than then, a reality that undercuts the assumptions on which the administration's analysis is based.

People do not become terrorists simply because they are born evil, hate our freedoms, or do not live in democracies. Instead, people commit acts of terror in response to their personal, political, and historical situations. Especially in the Islamic world, they harbor enormous resentment about the fate of their societies and their coreligionists, and they feel a great sense of frustration, humiliation, and injustice. Part of the humiliation is personal, often the result of alienation from living in foreign cultures. The terrorism expert Peter Bergen has pointed out that many of the top planners and pilots involved in 9/11 became more militant while living in the West, where "perceived discrimination, alienation and homesickness seem to have turned them all in a more radical direction."[13]

Beyond the personal alienation is a broader sense of victimization and shame at the fate of Islamic civilization—in a culture in which both pride and sense of community play even more important roles than elsewhere. A once great Islamic civilization, famous for its scientists, scholars, and artists, has seen itself surpassed economically, politically, and culturally by its former colonial overlords, distant Asians, and even the local upstart, Israel. Many Muslims blame this civilizational decline on the West, which they see as having broken up, occupied, and colonized Muslim lands.

Osama bin Laden has often underscored the role of Muslim humiliation in explaining and justifying the 9/11 at-

tacks. Just three weeks after 9/11, in his first public statement, bin Laden said, "What America is tasting now is
something insignificant compared to what we have tasted
for scores of years. Our nation [the Islamic world] has been
tasting this humiliation and this degradation for eighty years.
Its sons are killed, its blood is shed, its sanctuaries are attacked and no one hears and no one heeds."[14] Al Qaeda's recruiting videos successfully play to this sense of injustice
and humiliation in their efforts to persuade young Muslims
to join the cause.[15]

In April 2006, the National Intelligence Estimate on
global terrorism summarized the underlying factors behind
the spread of the jihadist movement. These factors did not
include hatred for freedom, desire for democracy, or the absence of Western resolve but "entrenched grievances, such
as corruption, injustice, and fear of Western domination,
leading to anger, humiliation, and a sense of powerlessness;
the Iraq jihad; the slow pace of real and sustained economic, social, and political reforms in many Muslim majority nations; and perceived anti-U.S. sentiment among most
Muslims—all of which jihadists exploit."[16] Similarly, MI5,
the British domestic intelligence service, underscores that it
was this sense of injustice and anger at British foreign
policy—and not the absence of democracy in Britain—that
was behind the July 2005 attacks on the London Underground. "The video wills of British suicide bombers," observed Dame Eliza Manningham-Buller, the head of MI5, in
November 2006, "make it clear that they are motivated by
perceived worldwide and longstanding injustices against
Muslims; an extreme and minority interpretation of Islam
promoted by some preachers and people of influence; and

their interpretation as anti-Muslim of UK foreign policy, in particular the UK's involvement in Iraq and Afghanistan."[17]

The perception of foreign occupation of Muslim lands also seems to contribute to terrorists' decisions to carry out attacks. The scholar Robert Pape showed in a recent study that in fact suicide bombers are far more often motivated by a desire to fight against foreign military occupation and for self-determination rather than by a desire to promote democracy at home. Looking at Tamil, Palestinian, Chechen, Kurdish, and al Qaeda suicide bombers, Pape found that what they most had in common was a perception that their communities were being humiliated by more powerful outsiders, and that they could reverse that humiliation by inflicting pain on those countries and obliging them to withdraw.[18]

None of this means that the United States should simply change its policies to make potential terrorists happy. But to deny any link between political context and an individual's decision to become a terrorist, or to willfully misplace blame on a vague hatred for freedom or lack of democracy, is to start the war on terror with a huge disadvantage. It is hard to fight an enemy without being honest about its real nature.

MISUSING FORCE

Even more misguided than the Bush administration's misstatement of the problem is its assumption that demonstrating toughness and deploying military force are keys to solving it. From the start, Bush declared that the new war would "not be won on the defensive," and in the ensuing months and years he proceeded to flesh out a military strategy based on anticipating and preempting potential threats.[19] The strategy, codified in the National Security Strategy of September 2002 and implemented in Iraq, is to "find and destroy" terrorists abroad "so that we do not have to face them in our own country."[20] "The only path to safety," Bush often argues, "is the path of action."[21] He insists that "you do not create terrorism by fighting terrorism."[22]

But though the United States might not be "creating terrorism," it is certainly creating conditions that generate more, rather than less, of it. The United States has had numerous successful operations against terrorists since 9/11, both military and judicial. Yet by invading and occupying Iraq, indefinitely detaining prisoners at Guantánamo Bay, endorsing and applying methods of interrogation widely considered to be torture, refusing to apply the Geneva Conventions, unreservedly justifying any Israeli military action as a necessary part of the global war on terror, and failing to prevent or punish those responsible for the atrocities in Iraqi prisons like Abu Ghraib, the United States has reinforced the grievances that inspire people to become terrorists, negating its efforts to kill or capture as many terrorists as possible. Contrary to Bush's apparent assumption that there is a fixed number of terrorists to be dealt with through death or arrest, in reality there is a vast pool of potential terrorist recruits, and any strategy that intensifies their motivations will ultimately fail. The images of large numbers of Muslim civilians being killed, broadcast daily on Arab satellite television, risks making the problem worse.

It is easy for disappointed supporters of the administration like Newt Gingrich to argue that the reason our current strategy is "not wrong, but failing" is because it is not being applied vigorously enough; it is harder, however, to envision what a more vigorous application of that strategy would consist of. Even if the United States could muster the resources and resolve to fight what Gingrich calls "World War III," it is far from clear that even a strategy of invading and occupying major Muslim countries would take care of the problem. The attempt to implant a peaceful pro-Western democracy in Iraq does not recommend itself as a model for the rest of the region.

The Bush strategy is also based on the assumption that the very demonstration of resolve will help deter future attacks. It is an odd suggestion that people willing to die for their cause would be deterred by our greater willingness to kill them, but the president and his supporters have often asserted that America's failure to impress the terrorists in this way was what led to the 9/11 attacks in the first place. The terrorists, Bush has argued, "saw our response to the hostage crisis in Iran, the bombings in the Marine barracks in Lebanon, the first World Trade Center attack, the killing of American soldiers in Somalia, the destruction of two U.S. embassies in Africa, and the attack on the USS *Cole.* The terrorists concluded that we lacked the courage and character to defend ourselves, and so they attacked us."[23]

Vice President Cheney has also insisted that "the terrorists came to believe that they could strike America without paying any price. And so they continued to wage those attacks, making the world less safe and eventually striking the United States on 9/11."[24] Speaking to marines at Camp Lejeune in October 2005, the vice president listed the same examples of alleged American weakness as Bush, concluding that "time and time again, for the remainder of the 20th century, the terrorists hit America and America did not hit back hard enough." Cheney then quoted Bush's argument that "the only way the terrorists can win is if we lose our nerve and abandon our mission."

In ascribing blame for the 9/11 attacks to the failures of Presidents Carter, Reagan, and Clinton to respond vigorously to previous attacks, it is unclear what precisely Bush and Cheney are suggesting should have been done in these past cases. They do not say whether they believe Reagan should have ordered massive air strikes against Hezbollah targets—or even invaded and occupied Lebanon—after the Marine barracks were bombed in 1983. Nor do they suggest which military targets would have been worth pounding in response to the first World Trade Center attack, in 1993, or that they would have advocated sending an overwhelming number of troops to Somalia that same year. Indeed, the Somalia disaster took place because of a military operation to go after the warlord Mohamed Farah Aideed, presumably the sort of tough, retaliatory strategy Bush and Cheney have advocated. They sometimes do invoke Ronald Reagan's 1986 military strikes on Libya in retaliation for Muammar Qaddafi's sponsorship of terrorism, again presumably the type of action they recommend for other cases. But reliance on that case conveniently overlooks the fact that the military strikes did not put an end to Libyan sponsorship of terrorism—including the bombing *two years later* of Pan Am flight 103 over Lockerbie, Scotland, which killed 270 people—and that Libya got out of the terrorism business only after a decade of broadly imposed UN sanctions.[25] Rather, the Bush-Cheney argument is pinned on the view that "credibility" and "toughness" are the best ways to deter terrorist actions. One of Secretary of Defense Rumsfeld's favorite sayings was that "weakness is provocative."[26] But it turns out toughness can be provocative as well.

The Bush-Cheney emphasis on "credibility" may well apply to states or dictators who value their power and fear retaliation. Unfortunately, it is less relevant to Islamist terrorists who have no power and see U.S. military retaliation as a recruitment tool. Clearly, the terrorists in Iraq have not been cowed by the U.S. invasion; if anything, they are inspired. In Iraq in 2003, the United States presumably "hit them hard" enough—to use Cheney's formulation—with 150,000 troops, a "shock and awe" air campaign, and the arrests of thousands, but the terrorist threat has not gone away. Indeed, the U.S. invasion and occupation have turned Iraq into an enormous terrorist training and recruiting ground.[27] Iraq, bin Laden declared, has become a "golden opportunity" to start a "third world war" against "the crusader-Zionist coalition."[28] He has publicly admitted that his goal has been to "provoke and bait" the United States into "bleeding wars" throughout the Islamic world, to bankrupt it as the Soviet Union was bankrupted in Afghanistan.[29]

This problem can be seen in microcosm in the way the American military has conducted its operations. As journalist Thomas Ricks shows in *Fiasco,* his devastating analysis of U.S. military operations in Iraq, American troops often failed to appreciate the role of honor in Arab societies and adopted tactics (like kicking down doors in the middle of the night to seize suspected insurgents in their homes) that were guaranteed to provoke members of the suspects' families and tribes to vow retaliation, creating a vicious circle of violence.[30] Administration supporters such as William Kristol and Lewis Lehrman argued in 2004 that the United States and the United Kingdom had to "crush the insurgents in Iraq" because "decisive military victories in Iraq would be respected by Sunnis, Shiites and Kurds alike."[31] They failed to see the risk that doing so would not only be difficult but counterproductive. This was a key lesson drawn in the new U.S. Army counterinsurgency manual, adopted in December 2006, which states that "people who have been maltreated or have had close friends or relatives killed by the government, particularly by its security forces, may strike back at their attackers. Security force abuses and the social upheaval caused by collateral damage from combat can be major escalating factors for insurgencies."[32]

The pattern of brute force's inadequacy as a counterterrorism strategy is visible in other parts of the Muslim world as well. Israel has not hesitated over the years to take extensive military actions, including bombing and occupying southern Lebanon, invading West Bank cities, and carrying out targeted killings. Whereas in many cases these actions have succeeded in preventing terrorists from carrying out attacks, they have not extinguished the country's terrorist threat, which today is arguably as great as ever. Another, more extreme example can be seen in Russia's brutal counterinsurgency tactics in Chechnya, which go well beyond what most Americans would be prepared to contemplate. They have failed to bring about the terrorist capitulation that Bush implies would result from a more resolute approach. The Russians, Israelis, and Americans have consistently underestimated the tendency of military intervention and occupation to generate nationalist resentment and violent resistance.

Military power has its uses in fighting terrorism: it served America well in destroying al Qaeda bases in Afghanistan and in ousting the Taliban regime that backed the terrorists who struck America on 9/11. But the utility of such power is limited even where it works (such as Afghanistan), sometimes counterproductive (such as Iraq), and entirely irrelevant in dealing with other aspects of the terrorism problem, such as those emanating from poor Muslim neighborhoods in Brixton or Madrid.

America cannot be shy about eliminating those who wish to do it harm. But it is simply not true, as Bush asserts, that "the only way the terrorists can win is if we lose our nerve and abandon our mission." They can also win if the United States becomes trapped in the obsessive pursuit of demonstrating resolve and loses sight of the fact that, in the long run, force alone is insufficient to defeat its enemies.

SQUANDERING CREDIBILITY

The outpouring of international sympathy for and solidarity with the United States following 9/11 was never going to last forever. America was the focus of a great deal of resentment before the attacks, and combating the terrorist threat was inevitably going to entail difficult decisions, some of which were likely to provoke further anger and resentment. What was not inevitable, however, was that the administration would react to those attacks by taking the view that the

United States had a blank check to do whatever it wanted in the name of national security, without abiding by traditional checks and balances or international law. By doing so, the administration did tremendous damage to America's credibility and moral authority, undermining allied support for the United States and fueling support for the terrorists in the Muslim world.

The erosion of U.S. moral standing did not result from a single policy, scandal, or transgression but rather from the accumulation of actions and decisions that have damaged the country's long-standing image as an example to others. Even a partial listing of these actions underscores the extent of the problem.

★ In January 2002, the administration decided to declare as "unlawful combatants" all prisoners captured in Afghanistan—with no rights under the Geneva Conventions. In many cases simply taking the word of Pakistani and Afghan allies who had taken the prisoners after the fall of Kabul (only a small fraction of the prisoners were arrested by U.S. forces), President Bush rejected appeals from the United Nations High Commissioner for Refugees to hold status-determination hearings, and he similarly rejected State Department support for applying the Geneva Conventions.[33] Many of these prisoners were then held at a prison on the U.S. naval base at Guantánamo Bay, Cuba, for the purpose, as a leading British judge later put it, of putting them "beyond the rule of law, beyond the protection of any courts, and at the mercy of the victors."[34]

★ In August 2002, lawyers in the Justice Department sought to redefine torture in a way that would give U.S. interrogators liberty to practice it without fear of prosecution. They argued that torture only occurred if it led to pain that was "excruciating and agonizing"; if it resulted "in significant psychological harm of significant duration, e.g., lasting for months or even years"; and if the person accused of torture had acted "with the *express purpose* of inflicting severe pain or suffering."[35] Moreover, the U.S. lawyers insisted that even if a person *had* committed torture under all of these narrow definitions, he would still not be guilty if his actions had been directed by the president, who as commander in chief had the authority to order whatever interrogation technique he wanted.[36]

★ In March 2003, the United States invaded Iraq in the face of significant international opposition. In its determination to overthrow Saddam Hussein, the Bush administration made ostentatious claims about weapons of mass destruction that turned out to be false, alleged links between Iraq and al Qaeda that did not exist, berated allies for refusing to back an invasion they argued would be unwise, and carried out that invasion without a viable plan for what to do if it produced chaos, civil war, and terrorism, which it did. The United States was hardly the only country to have been wrong about the status of Iraq's weapons of mass destruction programs, but by creating a false sense of urgency based on exaggerated claims, President Bush and other administration officials inevitably lost an enormous amount of credibility when no weapons were found.

★ From 2002 until 2004, the Bush administration denied attempts by prisoners held at Guantánamo—U.S. citizens and noncitizens alike—to challenge their detention in court. On June 28, 2004, however, the Supreme Court issued two opinions—*Rasul v. Bush* and *Hamdi v. Rumsfeld*—that overturned this practice.[37] In the latter case, Justice Sandra Day O'Connor felt obliged to remind the administration that the Supreme Court had "long since made clear that a state of war is not a blank check for the president when it comes to the rights of the nation's citizens."[38]

★ In April 2004, news reports revealed that U.S. soldiers and prison guards had been systematically abusing Iraqi detainees at the Abu Ghraib prison outside of Baghdad.[39] The abuses had come to the attention of the army months earlier but were not made public or ended until they were revealed by the press. As documented in photographs published around the world, the practices used at the prison included mock executions, use of attack dogs, sexual humiliation, forcing prisoners to assume painful "stress" positions, and severe physical beatings, some of which resulted in the death of prisoners.[40] Although a number of low-level soldiers were court-martialed for these abuses, no senior military officials, CIA personnel, or political leaders were held accountable.[41] The administration subsequently acknowledged that Secretary of Defense Rumsfeld had authorized the use of similar techniques in Guantánamo, yet continued to deny that the abuses in Iraq stemmed from official policy.

★ In early 2005, Senator John McCain of Arizona sought to put an end to prisoner abuse and restore America's reputation with a proposed amendment to a defense authorization bill prohibiting "cruel, inhuman and degrading treatment" of any detainee held by any U.S. authorities. Despite McCain's standing on the issue—he was a former prisoner of war who had been tortured in a North Vietnamese prison—and the strong support he received in Congress, the administration vigorously resisted the amendment, Vice President Cheney lobbied to exempt CIA operatives from the ban on "cruel, inhuman and degrading treatment," and President Bush threatened a veto.[42] Although the McCain amendment was overwhelmingly approved by the Congress, President Bush's "signing statement" on December 30, 2005, explained that he would construe the new law "in a manner consistent with the constitutional authority of the President to supervise the unitary executive branch and as Commander-in-Chief and consistent with the constitutional limitations on the judicial power."[43] In other words, the president did not recognize a congressional or judicial right to constrain his ability to authorize interrogations as he saw fit, so he would simply ignore the law of the land.

★ In late 2005, the *Washington Post* revealed that the CIA was maintaining secret camps in at least eight countries where prisoners were being held without having been charged and free from any international or judicial oversight. The Bush administration initially refused to admit the existence of such camps and sought to punish those who passed the information to the press. Eventually,

President Bush had to admit that the reports were true and acknowledged that the prisoners were being held abroad to allow the CIA to use "enhanced" interrogation procedures that would not have been allowed within the United States.[44] Senior officials like Attorney General Alberto Gonzales had to explain that while it was U.S. policy not to torture, there was "no legal prohibition" on the use of cruel, inhuman, and degrading treatment by U.S. personnel on detainees held abroad.[45]

★ In June 2006, the Supreme Court ruled (in *Hamdan v. Rumsfeld*) that the president had exceeded his constitutional authority by not consulting Congress when he created military commissions to try terrorist suspects. The Court also ruled that Common Article 3 of the Geneva Conventions, which prohibits "outrages upon personal dignity" and "humiliating and degrading treatment," should have been applied to all prisoners in U.S. custody and also called into question the legality of the administration's secret CIA detention program. In response, the administration sought to persuade Congress to authorize military commissions almost identical to those the Court had challenged and to "redefine" Common Article 3 in a way that would give U.S. interrogators more leeway. A group of senators led by McCain, Lindsey Graham of South Carolina (a former military judge), and John Warner of Virginia (a former chairman of the Armed Services Committee) refused to modify Common Article 3. After a bitter and complicated negotiation, Congress passed the Military Commissions Act on September 28, 2006. The legislation gave the administration most of what it wanted, including the ban on detainees using the writ of habeas corpus to challenge their detention, the potential use of evidence obtained through cruel, inhuman, or degrading treatment, and the use of hearsay evidence in trials.

The culmination of all these policies and practices—along with others such as warrantless wiretapping, "renditions" of prisoners to countries that practice torture, and CIA kidnappings in allied countries—has severely damaged America's reputation as a country that respects human rights and the rule of law. It would be hard to think of a greater gift that could have been given to al Qaeda recruiters who prey on Muslim perceptions of bias and mistreatment.

CONFLATING THREATS

Another serious misconception of the current American approach is the failure to recognize the differences within the Islamic world. George W. Bush's war on terror seems to be directed simultaneously at the most diverse of enemies—the Sunni Islamist al Qaeda network; Shiite Arab extremist groups such as Hezbollah; a Shiite Persian state in Iran; secular Sunni autocrats in countries like Egypt and Saudi Arabia; the Islamist group Hamas as well as the secular Palestinian Fatah; the minority Alawite regime in Syria; and various Muslim extremist groups in Europe or in the wider Muslim world. Many of these groups are actually enemies of one another, even as they are enemies of the United States: Iran and al Qaeda are bitter rivals; Shiite and Sunni groups in Iraq are engaged in violent combat; al Qaeda's primary goal is to topple the Sunni autocrats; and Fatah and Hamas are adversaries who have practically waged war against each other.

Each of these diverse groups poses, in its own way, real problems for the United States, but lumping them together into an undifferentiated "enemy" violates all the basic principles of good strategy. It makes it impossible for American policymakers to prioritize among threats, allocate resources, play adversaries off one another, and distinguish between urgent threats requiring action and less serious problems that can be contained. Even worse, as the French scholar Olivier Roy has pointed out, failing to disaggregate the aims and motivations of such groups, however objectionable each might be in its own right, "plays directly into the hands of the Iranian leaders and of bin Laden, who want . . . to tie all the existing conflicts together into a 'global jihad.'"[46]

The tendency to lump all these diverse issues into a single "war on terror" started early, with President Bush's division of the world into those who were "with us" and those who were "with the terrorists." Soon thereafter, Bush identified an "Axis of Evil" that consisted of three countries that had wildly divergent interests and agendas. The trio of Iraq, Iran, and North Korea may well have been evil, but in no way was it an "axis." None of the three, moreover, had anything to do with the 9/11 attacks.

Nor did it take long for the administration to begin conflating the different problems of states and terrorist groups. Influential senior officials such as Deputy Secretary of Defense Paul Wolfowitz were determined from the start to find and demonstrate an Iraqi role behind the 9/11 attacks.

As early as September 13, 2001, Wolfowitz vowed that the United States would focus on "removing the sanctuaries, removing the support systems, ending states who sponsor terrorism," and later that month he sent the former CIA director James Woolsey to London to investigate Iraq's possible role in 9/11.[47] Wolfowitz, Woolsey, and fellow neo-conservative thinker Richard Perle would later endorse a widely discredited thesis that Iraq was behind the first World Trade Center attack.[48] In his famous prediction that the war against Iraq would be a "cakewalk," Ken Adelman of Rumsfeld's Defense Policy Board claimed that such an operation "would constitute the greatest victory in America's war on terrorism."[49] Undersecretary of Defense for Policy Douglas Feith, who would later be put in charge of security planning for postwar Iraq, noted that the link between terrorist organizations and state sponsors became the "principal strategic thought underlying our strategy in the war on terrorism."[50]

Yet that "principal strategic thought" seemed to be largely beside the point. Iraq had nothing to do with 9/11, Iran and al Qaeda were and would remain enemies, and the terrorists who would attack in places like London, Bali, and Madrid were relatively independent actors who had little or no support from states. Support from countries like Iraq, Iran, and Syria for terrorist groups such as Hamas, Hezbollah, and the al Aqsa Martyrs Brigade existed and was and is a real problem. But it was and is a very different problem— requiring a different type and level of response—from the one that led to the 9/11 terrorist attacks.

The Iraq war, of course, was an even more egregious conflation of separate problems. Bush often spoke as if Iraq and the "war on terror" were the same problem, talking repeatedly about 9/11 when making the case for invading Iraq. Consequently, even four years after 9/11, nearly half of all Americans still believed that Iraq—and Saddam Hussein personally—were behind the attacks.[51] On the eve of the Iraq war, Wolfowitz most clearly stated the case for linkage: "The weapons of mass terror and the terrorist networks with which Iraq is in league are not two distinct threats. They are part of the same threat. The disarmament of Iraq and the war on terrorism are not only connected. Depriving Iraq of its chemical and biological weapons of mass destruction, and dismantling its nuclear weapons development program, is crucial to victory in the war against terrorism."[52]

Years later, after Saddam Hussein had been removed from power and no relevant links with al Qaeda had been found, the Bush administration was still insisting that Saddam Hussein's links with terrorism justified the invasion of Iraq. Witness Vice President Cheney in September 2006, when challenged on such linkage: "I'm not sure what part you don't understand here. In . . . 1990, the State Department designated Iraq as a state sponsor of terror. Abu Nidal, famous terrorist, had sanctuary in, in Baghdad for years. [Abu-Musab al-]Zarqawi was in Baghdad after we took Afghanistan and before we went into Iraq. You had the facility up at Kermal, poisons facility, run by Ansar Islam, an affiliate of al Qaeda. You had the fact that Saddam Hussein, for example, provided payments to the families of suicide bombers of $25,000 on a regular basis. This was a state sponsor of terror. He had a relationship with terror groups. No question about it. Nobody denies that."[53]

Cheney's examples, then, were a Palestinian terrorist

from the 1970s and 1980s who apparently went to Iraq in 1999 and died there in 2002; a Jordanian terrorist who went to Iraq in 2002 to prepare to fight against the pending U.S. invasion; a Kurdish terrorist group operating in the part of Iraq that was controlled by America's anti-Saddam Hussein allies; and Saddam's support for Palestinian terrorists. That all of these individuals and groups were despicable was unarguable. That they stood alongside Saddam Hussein as central actors in a single, global war on terror, however, was a fantasy, and the idea that they provided a good justification for the costs and risks of invading and occupying Iraq was preposterous. There were always serious reasons to argue that invading Iraq might be necessary—nuclear weapons concerns, humanitarian concerns, a desire to ensure respect for UN Security Council resolutions, and even the hope of trying to provoke political change and democracy in the Middle East. But the argument that Iraq had a direct link to the "global war on terror" and to those who had attacked the United States on 9/11 was a grave distortion that misled many Americans into believing that the war was worth the risks.

The conflation of diverse threats has also been a problem elsewhere in the Middle East. The Shiite Islamist group Hezbollah in Lebanon, for example, has certainly committed terrorist atrocities and is a declared enemy of America's ally Israel. But even though Hezbollah receives money and weapons from Iran and Syria, it also has predominantly local motivations and aims that are not only different from, but are in strong contrast to, those of the region's autocratic Sunni states and global terrorist groups like al Qaeda. Yet when Hezbollah attacked Israel in the summer of 2006, killing eight and capturing two Israeli soldiers, Bush declared the attack to be part of the global war on terror, placing it alongside Afghanistan and Iraq as one of three main fronts.[54] Commentators like former Speaker of the House Newt Gingrich and Senator Rick Santorum began talking about "World War III," and lumping Hezbollah together with al Qaeda, Iran, North Korea, Saudi Arabia, and others as the enemy in this global war.[55]

This line of thinking ignored not only the many differences among these groups but, more important, it ignored that the challenge from Shiite Hezbollah was initially viewed with as much concern in the Sunni Arab world as it was in Israel. At an Arab League summit meeting in Cairo in July 2006, representatives of the Sunni governments of Saudi Arabia, Jordan, Egypt, and several Persian Gulf states chastised Hezbollah for "unexpected, inappropriate and irresponsible acts," and Prince Saud al-Faisal, the Saudi foreign minister, said that Hezbollah's attacks on Israel would "pull the whole region back to years ago, and we cannot simply accept them."[56] Instead of taking advantage of the divisions in the Muslim world and the potential for Sunni resistance to the Hezbollah threat, America offered unreserved support for a poorly conceived Israeli bombing campaign that had unattainable objectives and produced high casualties among Arab civilians. This had serious costs. It drove Sunnis and Shiites together in an anti-American front, it enhanced Hezbollah's status within Lebanon and throughout the Muslim world, it made the task of Arab reformers that much harder, and it undermined America's potential role as an honest broker between Israel and its neighbors.

The same problem plagues the administration's approach

to the Palestinian group Hamas. Iranian and Syrian support for Hamas exists and is a serious impediment to peace because Hamas uses some of that aid to conduct attacks on Israeli civilians. But this should not obscure the fact that Hamas's origins—and the explanation of its electoral success—are to be found not in the global Islamist movement but in the nationalist Palestinian struggle and the resentment of the corruption and failures of Yasser Arafat's Fatah movement. Ironically, Fatah was often described as part of the same "global war on terror" even while it was practically at war with Hamas. During armed clashes between the two groups in late 2006, Fatah supporters taunted Hamas militants with cries of "Shi'a! Shi'a!" underscoring the growing depth of the sectarian divide in the Middle East and the absurdity of considering Hamas and Fatah as part of the same single "enemy."[57] While Hamas's appeal to Islamist themes and rhetoric is undeniable, to see and treat it primarily as part of a unified, global organization—and to conflate its aims and motivations with those of other, very different groups—risks becoming a self-fulfilling prophecy.

Despite all the evidence to the contrary, in his 2007 State of the Union address Bush was still referring to "the enemy" (singular) and insisting that "the Shiite and Sunni extremists are different faces of the same totalitarian threat." He implied that his efforts at democracy promotion had been proceeding well during 2005, and only ran into trouble when "a thinking enemy watched all of [the progress], adjusted their tactics and in 2006 they struck back."[58] But in reality, as Glenn Kessler noted in the *Washington Post,* "his description of the actions of 'the enemy' tried to tie together a series of diplomatic and military setbacks that had virtually no connection to one another, from an attack on a Sunni mosque in Iraq to the assassination of [a] Maronite Lebanese political figure."[59]

The case for acting militarily against any particular threat can be made, but it should be made on its merits and not on the misguided notion that such action is part of a single, global war. Otherwise, U.S. policy will only continue to drive diverse enemies together rather than take advantage of opportunities to pull them apart.

ALIENATING ALLIES

To fight what was being called a global war, one might have thought a premium would be placed on the construction of a global alliance. But President Bush and his supporters from the start underestimated both the importance and the difficulty of building such an alliance and based their efforts to do so on a very specific—and highly flawed—conception of leadership. They believed that American power and morality were so clearly evident that all the United States had to do was to chart a bold course and its allies would be likely to follow.

"I'm amazed that there is such misunderstanding of what our country is about," Bush remarked in October 2001. "Like most Americans, I just can't believe it. Because I know how good we are."[60] But in fact, even America's closest allies did not automatically assume its intentions to be pure, and America's undoubted power created much resistance around the world, even among those who tended to follow Washington's lead.

Bush's vision of American leadership had been developed and articulated well before 9/11. Indeed, as a presidential candidate in 2000, Bush specifically campaigned on the notion that the Clinton administration had been far too deferential to other countries' sensibilities in formulating its foreign policies. The new administration's vision was that important U.S. foreign policy goals could only be realized through decisive American leadership and, if necessary, through unilateral action. Such leadership entailed staking out firm positions and then demonstrating the capacity and determination to follow through regardless of opposition. The administration was convinced that U.S. allies and partners would eventually follow the American lead and simultaneously allow the United States to maintain its freedom of action. The argument was that multilateralism had to be "preceded by unilateralism," otherwise the followers would never follow.[61]

Bush started to implement this vision of leadership immediately upon taking office, by rejecting international accords on climate change, ballistic missile defense, and the International Criminal Court. But it was 9/11 that seemed to convince him that the stakes were now too high to allow foreigners to influence U.S. decisions about its vital interests. As he declared the war on terror, Bush made clear that he welcomed allies who wanted to join him, but also that he would not be prepared to compromise to win their support. "At some point we may be the only ones left," Bush said in the fall of 2001. "That's okay with me. We are America."[62]

The problem is, more than six years into the war on terror, in some ways we are just about the only one left. Launching the war in Iraq, Bush insisted that "we really don't need anybody's permission" to defend our security, and of course that was true.[63] But by neglecting diplomacy, ignoring the foreign policy priorities of allies, mistreating detainees, launching the invasion of Iraq in the face of stiff international opposition, and accusing opponents of the war of disloyalty if not dishonesty, the administration has alienated friends and potential allies around the globe.

According to the Pew Global Attitudes Project, between 2002 and 2006 the percentage of people with a "favorable opinion" of the United States fell dramatically: from 75 to 56 percent in the United Kingdom; from 63 to 39 percent in France; from 61 to 37 percent in Germany; from 61 to 43 percent in Russia; from 61 to 30 percent in Indonesia; from 25 to 15 percent in Jordan; and from 30 to 12 percent in Turkey.[64] Also according to Pew, the number of respondents who believed that the United States took their country's interests into account was 38 percent in Germany; 32 percent in the United Kingdom; 21 percent in Russia; 20 percent in the Netherlands; 19 percent in Spain; 19 percent in Canada; 18 percent in France; 17 percent in Jordan; 14 percent in Turkey; and 13 percent in Poland.[65] By the end of 2006, an average of only 29 percent of people polled in eighteen different countries had a "mainly positive" view of the United States, a level that had fallen from 36 percent earlier in 2006 and 40 percent in 2005.[66]

In the Arab world, America's standing was even lower. According to a 2006 poll conducted in six Arab countries (Egypt, Jordan, Lebanon, Morocco, Saudi Arabia, and the

United Arab Emirates), 57 percent of those polled had a "very unfavorable" view of the United States, with 21 percent more "somewhat unfavorable," and only 12 percent either "somewhat favorable" or "very favorable." In the same poll, 38 percent named George W. Bush as the foreign leader they most disliked (for the first time outpacing two Israeli prime ministers, Ariel Sharon at 11 percent and Ehud Olmert at 7 percent), while Hezbollah leader Hassan Nasrallah was the foreign leader most admired at 14 percent, followed by French president Jacques Chirac at 8 percent and Iranian president Mahmoud Ahmadinejad at 4 percent. When asked which country they would most like to see as the world's sole superpower, 19 percent said France; 16 percent said China; 14 percent said Pakistan; 10 percent said Germany; and only 8 percent said the United States. Seventy-two percent of the Arabs polled said that they considered the United States the greatest threat to world peace; 36 percent saw France as the country with the most freedom and democracy, compared to just 14 percent for the United States.[67]

In 2003, newspaper columnist Max Boot, a Bush supporter, argued that "resentment comes with the territory."[68] And William Kristol of the *Weekly Standard* concluded: "We need to err on the side of being strong. . . . And if people want to say we're an imperial power, fine."[69] But it turns out not to be so fine. In an age of democracies, global resentment makes it harder for leaders to cooperate with the United States, and harder for America to achieve its goals throughout the world.

THE RESOURCE GAP

Finally, one of the oddest aspects of the Bush approach has been the enormous gap between the rhetoric of war and the resources devoted to it. From the moment Bush declared a war on terror, he has implied it was an existential threat to the United States—"a threat with no precedent"—and required the most exceptional measures in response. The war on terror would "begin with al Qaeda" but it "would not end until every terrorist group of global reach has been found, stopped, and defeated," he said.[70] By talking of global war, invoking Winston Churchill and Franklin Roosevelt, accusing critics of "appeasement," and warning of the threat from "Islamic fascists," Bush and other administration officials did not hesitate to compare the current conflict to the greatest war of all.[71] At one point Rumsfeld even compared the defenders of the president's policies to those in the 1930s who were "ridiculed or ignored" by people who "argued that the fascist threat was exaggerated or that it was someone else's problem."[72]

The terrorists who attacked the United States on 9/11 were certainly dangerous, and just how great a danger Islamist extremism poses to America and the world is a legitimate debate. And at least some who argue, like Gingrich, that America is now engaged in a third world war are willing to call for resources commensurate with the threat. The administration, on the other hand, talks about world wars, but refused (until January 2007) to increase the size of the military, has cut more than $1.5 trillion in taxes, and spends roughly 4 percent of the GDP on defense—about half the average defense spending as a share of the economy as during the Cold

War. In World War II, by way of comparison, the United States mobilized 16 million men, operated a draft, and spent nearly 40 percent of the GDP on defense. On January 10, 2007, Bush proclaimed that the war in Iraq would "determine the direction of the global war on terror—and our safety here at home," yet he called for a troop increase for that war of less than 22,000 troops—to be accomplished by extending existing tours of duty and accelerating deployments, not by calling up more soldiers. The gap between rhetoric and response suggests that Bush himself may not believe that the threat is as great as he claims, and it breeds cynicism among those who believe that the "war" is being used for political ends.

We will never know if Bush's critics like Gingrich and Kristol are right when they say that the war on terror could have been won and could still be salvaged with enough resources, which they claim would enable America to win in Iraq, destroy terrorist enemies, and intimidate Syria and Iran. There are reasons to doubt it. But at least these critics are consistent and willing to call for an alignment of ends and means. To have a strategy based on transforming the greater Middle East and deterring and destroying all our enemies, but not backing that strategy with adequate means, was a recipe for failure from day one.

★ ★ ★

There was nothing inevitable about the wrong war. The 9/11 terrorist attacks and the dangers they revealed posed a tremendous challenge to the United States, and none of the choices were easy or solutions obvious. But this was not the first time we faced a serious, multifaceted threat, and not the first time our leaders had to find the right dose of offense, defense, ideology, military strength, and patience to lead the country to safety. In another, not so distant era, American leaders were also faced with unprecedented and deadly challenges, and they did a better job.

2 ★ HOW WE WON THE COLD WAR

If you think America faces big challenges today, consider how the world looked to Harry Truman. Sixty years ago, this modest Missourian, who had never expected to be president, found himself facing a set of global challenges that must have appeared even more daunting than ours today. Having defeated Nazi Germany and Imperial Japan, the United States found itself facing a rising threat of an entirely different character. Stalin's Soviet Union was not only a massive, expansionist, militarized, hostile, industrial state, but it was also at the head of a communist movement whose expressed aim was to destroy international capitalism and spread its ideology around the world.

In the wake of communism's eventual demise, that aim seems implausible, but it certainly seemed realistic at the time. In 1947, communist advances in Greece and Turkey—and a bankrupt Great Britain's inability to fight them—led the president to announce what quickly became known as the Truman Doctrine, pledging the United States to resist communist aggression and "support free peoples who are resisting attempted subjugation by armed minorities or by outside pressures."[1] In Eastern Europe, what Churchill had dubbed the "Iron Curtain" now descended "from Stettin in the Baltic to Trieste on the Adriatic," and Moscow made clear it had no intention of coexisting with democratic movements in its sphere of influence.[2] As if to prove that point, in February 1948, Stalin's communist allies in Czechoslovakia seized power in a coup during which the pro-Western, democratic leader Jan Masaryk jumped—or more likely was pushed—to his death from a window in the foreign ministry. In China, Mao Zedong's communists were on their way to defeating America's ally Chiang Kai-shek, who by 1949 would be driven off the mainland to Taiwan. After twenty-five years of civil war, the world's most populous country was now in the hands of radical Marxist-Leninists who were siding with Moscow and loudly pronouncing their goal of spreading the communist revolution. From Iran to Vietnam to Guatemala to Cuba to Indonesia to Egypt, significant communist parties threatened to take power, and not necessarily through the ballot box. *Time* magazine in 1949 worried about "the red tide that threatens to engulf the world."[3] In June 1950, when 135,000 North Korean troops suddenly crossed the thirty-eighth parallel in an attempt to unify the Korean peninsula under the communist banner, it seemed to many like the start of a potential third world war.

In some ways even more worrisome than communism's expansionism—for at least that could be resisted through force of arms, and the United States was still the most powerful country in the world—was the insidious nature of the communist threat. To many around the world, especially in developing countries, where income inequality and colonialism had bred enormous resentment, the appeal of commu-

nism was powerful and easy to understand. Marxism offered a "scientific" theory about how capitalism would inevitably fail, and promised a nirvana of brotherly solidarity
and world peace. As capitalism left some people behind and
left others unsatisfied with material advancement alone, the
prospect of a Marxist revolution gave idealists around the
world something to believe in and fight and die for. Even in
free, advanced Western democracies like France and Italy,
large and well-organized communist parties represented
more than a quarter of the electorate, and in both cases
were slavishly loyal to Moscow and the aims of the Third International.

Within the United States, where communism had not
taken hold, it was not only the paranoid or ultranationalistic
who feared that the ideology could spread, especially if capitalism entered one of its periodic crises. The 1950 McCar-
ran Act, passed by Congress over Truman's veto, stated:
"World Communism has as its sole purpose the establish-
ment of a totalitarian dictatorship in America, to be brought
about by treachery, infiltration, sabotage and terrorism."
The rhetoric was overblown and led to some disgraceful
witch hunts, but it also reflected genuine fears based on the
reality that foreign communists actually did want to undermine the United States, and there were those within the
country willing to help them. In January 1950, the former
State Department official Alger Hiss was convicted of per-
jury for denying having been a Soviet spy in the 1930s and
1940s, and three days later, the British government revealed
that Klaus Fuchs, an émigré German scientist, had con-
fessed to turning over nuclear weapons secrets to Moscow.[4]
In May 1951, two other British spies, Donald Maclean and

Guy Burgess, were unmasked as Soviet agents and defected to Moscow before they could be arrested. Many Americans wondered how many of their compatriots or allies were secretly working for the other side.

The specter of a growing communist threat was hardly a passing phenomenon. By 1949, the Soviet Union possessed nuclear weapons, and by 1952 it had tested a thermonuclear bomb that would eventually give it the capability to obliterate large parts of the United States. Khrushchev's famous 1956 comment "We will bury you" was meant not as a prediction of war but as an expression of confidence that history was on Moscow's side, not America's, and many Americans believed him.[5] The 1957 launch of *Sputnik,* the first artificial satellite, seemed to confirm the Soviet Union's mounting technological superiority, and even in the West many started to believe Khrushchev's claim that "the socialist mode of production possesses decisive advantages over the capitalist mode."[6] We now know, of course, that the "socialist mode of production" was a catastrophic failure and that it was the Soviet system that would end up dead and buried. But that was not how it seemed at the time. Idealistic young people in Buenos Aires, Paris, Kinshasa, New York, and San Francisco wore Lenin or Che Guevara T-shirts and were sincere in believing that communism offered a better and more just future than the American model.

Coping with this kind of threat, Americans came to realize, would be different from anything America had faced in the past. Traditional war was effectively ruled out—modern technology and nuclear weapons made it almost impossible to contemplate—but the Cold War was nonetheless a struggle that would have to be fought and won. And that required an entirely new kind of war—one that would, from time to time, require fighting proxy battles with military means, but a war that would ultimately only be won when the enemy's ideology collapsed. Whereas World War II was decided in the mud around Stalingrad, on the beaches of Normandy, and in the radiated ruins of Hiroshima and Nagasaki, the Cold War would be decided in the hearts and minds of those waging it on both sides. It would not end with American forces occupying the Kremlin, but rather when the occupant of the Kremlin abandoned the fight, because the people he governed had stopped believing in the ideology they were supposed to be fighting for.

In this sense, it is the Cold War—far more than World War II or any other traditional war—that provides the most instructive metaphor for the struggle against Islamist terrorism today. Like the Cold War, the war on terror is not about destroying hostile armies but about destroying misguided dreams. Like the Cold War, it is multifaceted and will require a strategy for victory with strong political, economic, diplomatic, and psychological aspects as well as military components. Like the Cold War, it cannot be won by the United States alone but will require allies and the legitimacy their support conveys. Like the Cold War, it will last for years if not decades and will require resolve, patience, cool heads, and sometimes uncomfortable moral compromises. But also like the Cold War, it can ultimately be won with a long-term strategy of maintaining our strength, containing the threat, choosing our battles carefully, and outlasting the enemy. Just as we won the Cold War only when our adversaries essentially gave up on a bankrupt ideology, we will only win the war against Islamist terrorism when the same thing happens.

Drawing lessons from our victory in the Cold War does not mean adopting it as a precise model for the current struggle. Clearly, Islamic extremists today are different from the communist extremists of yesterday, and the Soviet Union was in many ways a cautious, deterrable state—like some states in the Middle East today, perhaps, though not like al Qaeda. The idea is not to try to replicate Cold War strategy, which in any case varied considerably over the decades, but rather to take advantage of some fundamental insights from the way America's leaders fought and won a long struggle against a vicious, determined, and seemingly insurmountable foe. There is much to learn from what we got wrong during the Cold War, and even more to learn from what we got right.

MANAGING THREATS

Americans, blessed with friendly and stable neighbors, protected by two oceans, and possessed of the power to defend themselves in a dangerous world, are not accustomed to living with threats—they would much prefer to eliminate them entirely, and they have usually been able to do so. Other countries—the smaller European nation-states, for example—might have had to get used to living with vulnerability, but for Americans the feeling is alien. Even when a dangerous world threatened American interests, those threats were mostly far from American shores, and even so a powerful America eventually determined it had to eliminate, rather than accommodate, them.

This historical experience—relative invulnerability and the power to eliminate threats—is what made the specter of Soviet communism so daunting at the start of the Cold War. By 1947, hopes that the United States and the Soviet Union could somehow cooperate in the building of a peaceful new world order had mostly collapsed. Communists appeared to be everywhere—in Russia, Europe, Asia, and Latin America—and their prospects appeared to be bright. The movement was ruthless, violent, subversive, expansionist, and had a powerful state sponsor. The invulnerability Americans had hoped to restore with victory in World War II seemed anything but assured, yet war with the Soviet Union—or indeed the global communist movement—was not an option.

It was in this context that the American diplomat George F. Kennan came forward with his proposal for a strategy of containing, rather than acting to reverse, the communist threat. In his famous "Long Telegram" from Moscow of February 22, 1946, which he revised for publication (under the pseudonym X) as "The Sources of Soviet Conduct" in *Foreign Affairs* in July 1947, Kennan offered the fundamental insight that America needed a policy that lay somewhere between launching World War III and capitulating to the communists.[7] Soviet communism was indeed a serious, insidious threat and Russia's leaders were "committed fanatically to the belief that with [the United States] there can be no permanent *modus vivendi,* that it is desirable and necessary that the internal harmony of our society be disrupted, our traditional way of life be destroyed, the international authority of our state be broken." But that threat, he said, could be managed by maintaining a vigorous defense, applying counterpressure, and making efforts to win over the world's population—and eventually the Soviets themselves—to our side. What Kennan thus proposed was a strategy of "long-term, patient but firm and vigilant containment."

For a country not used to having to compromise strong moral principles and that had just fought a total war against pure evil, this was a radical—and not particularly appealing— suggestion. As the historian John Lewis Gaddis observed, Kennan's strategy of containment was innovative in that it "mapped out a path between dangerous—even deadly alternatives." Gaddis notes: "The dominant trend in thinking about strategy through the end of World War II was one of bipolar extremes: war *or* peace, victory *or* defeat, appeasement *or* annihilation. The idea that there could be something in between—neither war *nor* peace, neither victory *nor* defeat, neither appeasement *nor* annihilation—had never been clearly articulated."[8] Kennan's basic argument was the opposite of Vice President Dick Cheney's "one percent doctrine," the notion that if there is a one percent chance of terrorists getting a weapon of mass destruction the United States should act as if it were a certainty.[9] Instead Kennan's argument was based on the view that it can sometimes be better to live with risk and try to reduce it than to seek to eliminate it entirely.

In some quarters Kennan's idea was roundly condemned from the moment it was first suggested. The willingness not only to tolerate risk but also to accept moral compromise— because peacefully coexisting with communism also meant condemning millions of people to live under tyranny—was felt to be inconsistent with traditional American idealism. As early as January 1946, General Leslie Groves, the wartime commander of the Manhattan Project, argued that a "ruth-lessly realistic" U.S. policy would never "permit any foreign power with which we are not firmly allied, and in which we do not have absolute confidence, to make or possess atomic weapons," and that if such a country "started to make atomic weapons we would destroy its capacity to make them before it had progressed far enough to threaten us."[10] For the next several years, numerous politicians, journalists, generals, senators, scholars, and scientists advocated a policy of pre-ventive war, either to forestall development of a Soviet nu-clear weapon or to defeat Moscow while the nuclear balance was still in America's favor.[11]

The desire to preempt the Soviet bomb—or even to try to change the regime in Moscow altogether—was understand-able. The Soviet Union was a ruthless adversary, bent on destroying the capitalist system, led by authoritarian rulers whose actions could not be predicted. Even so, there is no evidence that any U.S. president ever seriously considered acting on that desire, because the risks of conventional con-flict were too great, and no one had a plan for what to do with Russia after the preventive war had been waged. In-deed, following a 1953 White House exercise to consider options for preventive war against Moscow, President Dwight Eisenhower concluded that the costs of such a policy would easily outweigh the benefits. "The colossal job of occupying the territories of the defeated enemy would be far beyond the resources of the United States at the end of such a war," he concluded.[12]

Also in the early 1950s, the Korean War provided an ob-ject lesson in how the search for absolute security—trying to eliminate threats rather than merely containing them—could end up creating more problems than it solved. When in June 1950 North Korea launched its surprise attack on the South, the invasion was widely (and wrongly) seen as a communist assault ordered by Moscow, possibly even a prelude to a Soviet attack on Western Europe. Taking advantage of the Soviet Union's empty seat on the UN Security Council (Moscow was boycotting the world body because of the exclusion of communist China), the Truman administration won UN authorization for a military intervention. The U.S. forces were led by General Douglas MacArthur, who managed to drive the North Koreans out of the South, following his risky and brilliant amphibious landing at Inchon in September 1950.

But MacArthur, not satisfied with having repelled and contained the North Koreans, then advocated destroying the North Korean regime altogether with an attack north of the thirty-eighth parallel. Despite the risk of Chinese intervention, he won the administration's reluctant support. When that risk turned into a reality—the Chinese sent nearly 300,000 troops across the Yalu River—U.S. and UN forces lost nearly all the territory they had gained. Despite the setback, MacArthur argued for expanding the war even further, to China itself and if necessary with the use of tactical nuclear weapons. When he resisted Truman's decision not to take this step, the president fired him for insubordination. In his famous farewell speech to Congress in April 1951, MacArthur insisted, "In war there is no substitute for victory," but his attempt to secure absolute victory in war had in fact turned out to be counterproductive.[13] The theory of eliminating threats to American security and affronts to American morality was as impeccable in 1950 as it was in

2003; the attempt to achieve those goals in practice was in both cases costly in terms of American lives, money, and reputation.

Discomfort with the containment doctrine, and with the necessity of living with the danger it required, endured for decades. In the 1952 presidential election campaign, the man who would become Eisenhower's secretary of state, John Foster Dulles, called for "the end of the negative, futile and immoral policy of 'containment,'" and he appealed for the "rollback" of communism in Eastern Europe.[14] Dulles wrote an article for *Life* magazine in which he criticized the Truman administration's "treadmill policies which, at best, might perhaps keep us in the same place until we drop exhausted."[15] In the 1960s, the conservative Republican senator and presidential candidate Barry Goldwater argued that "the most serious defect of all" in America's alliance system was that it was "completely defensive in nature and outlook." Goldwater argued, "As long as every encounter with the enemy is fought on his initiative, on grounds of his choosing and with weapons of his choosing, we shall keep on losing the Cold War."[16] In the 1970s, the neoconservative movement arose, as prominent intellectuals like Norman Podhoretz and Richard Pipes, emerging figures like Richard Perle and Paul Wolfowitz, and politicians like Senator Henry Jackson of Washington railed against the policy of détente with the Soviet Union and called for a more assertive and militarized approach to the Cold War. The reality, however, was that none of these critics ever really advocated serious alternatives to Kennan's essentially defensive strategy. "Historical patience," the political scientist Dana Allin has written, was "not one of the more conspicuous of American virtues." But once containment was adopted under Truman, "no later administration ever really took it upon itself to alter the fundamental defensiveness of U.S. policy."[17]

Containment did not exclude—indeed it required—large defense expenditures and the periodic willingness to use military force. In 1981, Ronald Reagan, a critic of containment, came to power and implemented an assertive version of the doctrine that saw the United States massively increase defense spending, confront its communist enemies militarily in places like Afghanistan, Angola, and Central America, and publicly question the Soviet Union's legitimacy. By forcing Moscow to spend even more money on defense, Reagan's policies arguably hastened the day when a Soviet leader would start looking for ways to end the Cold War. By the late 1980s, contrary to the assertions of growing Soviet strength made by many of Reagan's strongest supporters, Soviet power had considerably weakened and the inferiority of the communist system had been manifestly established. The ideological and material rot that Kennan had foreseen had set in, and the patience shown by two generations of American leaders had paid off. Living with the Soviet threat was not an ideal option for anyone, and the critics were always right to criticize containment as dangerous, morally suspect, and politically awkward. But for forty years it helped the United States avoid "World War III," and it made possible an unambiguous victory in the Cold War.

PRESERVING OUR VALUES

Another lesson from the Cold War is that preserving the virtues of our own society is a crucial tool in outlasting and defeating an enemy ideology. The notion that our enemy would defeat itself was an ironic twist on the Cold War, because it was Marx and Lenin who had claimed that capitalism would die of its own contradictions. But as John Lewis Gaddis has pointed out, "Kennan in the late 1940s and Reagan in the early 1980s reversed this logic, insisting that it was Marxism-Leninism, not capitalism, that carried within itself the seeds of its own destruction." The United States could "increase the strains under which the Soviet Union and its allies operated," Gaddis noted, but in the end communism would fail because of "the inefficiencies of command economics, the absence of political accountability, and the improbability that an internationalist ideology could indefinitely suppress nationalist instincts. . . . Americans and their allies needed only to be firm and remain patient while this happened."[18]

This was, in the end, what did happen to communism, and there is every reason to believe today that the extremist ideology America faces will also fail and die of its own contradictions. America again needs only to increase the strains under which it operates, avoid fueling its causes, defend itself in the meantime, and remain firm and patient while it happens.

Kennan advocated this sort of patience and self-confidence, stressing the need to keep our own house in order. He argued that the key to defeating the Soviet Union would be to maintain the "health and vigor of our own society." World communism, Kennan wrote, "is like [a] malignant parasite which feeds only on diseased tissue. This is the point at which domestic and foreign policies meet. Every courageous and incisive measure to solve internal problems of our own society, to improve self-confidence, discipline, morale, and community spirit of our own people is a diplomatic victory . . . worth a thousand diplomatic notes and joint communiqués." Kennan concluded, "We must have [the] courage and self-confidence to cling to our own methods and conceptions of human society. After all, the greatest danger that can befall us in coping with this problem . . . is that we shall allow ourselves to become like those with whom we are coping."[19]

Around the same time others also stressed the importance of maintaining our own democratic values and worried that we might not be able to do so in a struggle against an authoritarian adversary. In 1941, the political scientist Harold Lasswell expressed concern that an era of total war would lead to the development of what he called "garrison states." Lasswell's concern was that constant states of emergency and the need to organize for modern warfare would undermine democracy and lead states to put control of society in the hands of dictatorial military authorities.[20] Lasswell's ideas gained prominence after the war, notably in an influential 1947 survey of national security issues by the journalist Hanson Baldwin. Baldwin argued that preparation for total war would "distort and twist the body politic" not only "*after* a war . . . but *prior* to war. . . . How can we prepare for total war," he asked, "without becoming a 'garrison state' and destroying the very qualities and virtues and principles we originally set about to save?"[21]

Despite these widespread concerns, the United States never became anything like a garrison state. To be sure, successive administrations often used the national security imperative to justify various constraints on civil liberties and defend expansions of presidential authority. But dedication to the Constitution, an effective justice system, and a strong public commitment to personal freedom and the rule of law ensured that excesses like McCarthyism and Watergate were the exception and not the rule, and that any abuses justified by the Cold War paled in comparison with what took place on the other side. Nor, despite the development of what President Eisenhower called the "military-industrial complex," did the need to prepare for total war lead to the militarization of American democracy. Indeed, while defense spending rose dramatically during the Korean War to reach a level of just over 14 percent of the GDP, it fell gradually after that, averaging less than 8 percent from 1947 to 1988. Even at the height of the Reagan military buildup in 1987—when critics were arguing that America was suffering from "imperial overstretch"—defense spending was just 6 percent of the GDP, about one-fourth of the equivalent measure for the Soviet Union.[22]

In not allowing the United States to become a garrison state, American leaders made clear that they understood Kennan's admonition that winning the Cold War would entail winning hearts and minds, and that would be possible only if America and the West remained a prosperous and liberal pole of attraction for the people of the communist bloc. Good domestic policy, in other words, would prove to be good foreign policy as well.

Harry Truman certainly understood this point. He defended some of his liberal domestic policies in precisely these terms. When he acted in 1948 to integrate the military and outlaw segregation in interstate commerce, Truman recognized that "if we wish to inspire the people of the world whose freedom is in jeopardy, if we wish to restore hope to those who have already lost their civil liberties, if we wish to fulfill the promise that is ours, we must correct the remaining imperfections in our practice of democracy."[23] The Marshall Plan, launched in 1947, was also designed not only to help restart European economies but to demonstrate American generosity. And NSC-68, the 1950 national security strategy document that elaborated the doctrine of containment, also stressed the importance of "building a successfully functioning political and economic system in the free world. . . . Against an adversary which effectively affirmed the constructive and hopeful instincts of men and was capable of fulfilling their fundamental aspirations, the Soviet system might prove to be fatally weak."[24] As Truman's head of policy planning at the time, Kennan argued that every measure taken "to improve self-confidence, discipline, moral and community spirit is a diplomatic victory over Moscow."[25]

Dwight Eisenhower was similarly concerned about the potential foreign policy costs of domestic illiberalism, insisting, "We must not destroy what we are attempting to defend." If America had to "resort to anything resembling a garrison state," he argued, "then all that we are striving to defend would be weakened and, if long subjected to this kind of control, could disappear."[26] Eisenhower's fear, as Gaddis explains, was that "in the effort to contain an authoritarian adversary, the United States itself might become authoritarian, whether through the imposition of a command economy or through the abridgement of democratic procedures."[27] This was what led him to warn, in his famous farewell address to the nation in January 1961, against the rise of the military-industrial complex.[28]

By the late 1960s and 1970s, the United States seemed to be in danger of losing its domestic bearings. Lyndon Johnson had allowed his "Great Society" programs to be diverted by the Vietnam War, and Richard Nixon's abuse of presidential power in Watergate—which the president sought to justify on national security grounds—came close to crossing Eisenhower's threshold for "destroying what we were attempting to defend." Nixon's foreign policy of détente, moreover, seemed to be a recognition that though the Soviet Union may well have "mellowed," as Kennan predicted it would, it was hardly likely to disappear.

Yet even as all this was happening, and the balance of power appeared to be shifting in the direction of the Soviet Union, the communist system was eroding and the Western world was stronger than it seemed. America overcame its Watergate and Vietnam fiascos, and even a capitalist system in recession in the late 1970s was far stronger economically, and far more popular politically, than the Soviet empire. It simply took the optimism of a Ronald Reagan to notice and act on that premise. Even in the midst of the Western pessimism of the mid-1970s, Reagan was insisting, in echoes of Kennan, that communism was "a temporary aberration which will one day disappear from the earth because it is contrary to human nature."[29] He observed that the Western economies were vastly richer than the communist economies, and he foresaw what many others had lost sight of—that "citizen Ivan" could become an "unexpected ally" in the Cold War, if he started to resent the failings of his own government's system.[30]

Reagan's first National Security Directive as president called on the United States to force Moscow to "bear the brunt of its economic shortcomings, and to encourage long-term liberalizing and nationalist tendencies within the Soviet Union and allied countries."[31] In a famous address to the British parliament in June 1982, Reagan explicitly turned Marx on his head, predicting "a great revolutionary crisis . . . where the demands of the economic order are conflicting directly with those of the political order," but noting that this crisis was happening not in the capitalist world but in the communist world. The Soviet Union, Reagan said, "runs against the tide of history by denying human freedom and human dignity to its citizens" and "any system is inherently unstable that has no peaceful means to legitimize its leaders." Reagan called on the West to insist "that freedom is not the sole prerogative of a lucky few, but the inalienable and universal right of all human beings." He expressed hope that in the long term, "the march of freedom and democracy . . . will leave Marxism-Leninism on the ash heap of history."[32] The following spring, in a speech in Florida, Reagan called the Soviet Union "another sad bizarre chapter in human history whose last pages are now being written."[33]

The words and ideas were controversial, but the ash heap of history is precisely where Marxism-Leninism ended up. By maintaining its own essential decency and prosperity, the capitalist system showed its vast superiority, a reality that was perhaps even more apparent in the communist world than in the West. "Citizen Ivan" may not have risen up against leaders in Moscow directly, but citizens Lech, Vaclav, Vygaudas, Lothar, and others—who saw and envied Western wealth and freedom—did rise up, demanding similar opportunities for themselves. By the mid-1980s, these Eastern European revolutions from below were met in Moscow by a revolution from above, as the new Soviet leader, Mikhail Gorbachev, recognized that the communist system was dying. "We can't go on living like this," Gorbachev told his wife, Raisa, on the eve of his promotion to general secretary in 1985.[34] Even against an authoritarian adversary and under the threat of total war, the West had managed to "preserve the health and vigor" of its own society. And the bankrupt ideology it was fighting against simply collapsed.

WINNING FRIENDS AND ALLIES

Faced with an existential threat like the nuclear-armed Soviet Union, American presidents must have felt tempted at times to run the NATO alliance the way the Soviets ran the Warsaw Pact—with an iron fist that tolerated little dissent. But the United States successfully avoided that temptation throughout the Cold War, and the alliance was stronger because of it. Allies often resented American power and leadership, but on the whole they respected the United States and remained firmly in the Western camp. Washington was able to ask favors and commitments from its democratic alliance partners not only because those partners feared American power but also because they felt they were getting something in return. If America was an empire during the Cold War, it was an "empire by invitation," in the words of the Norwegian historian Geir Lundestad.[35]

The United States created a liberal security community in the immediate postwar period, but not because it lacked the power to rule in a more imperial fashion. Indeed, as

British politician Harold Laski wrote in 1947, "America bestrides the world like a colossus; neither Rome at the height of its power nor Great Britain in the period of economic supremacy enjoyed an influence so direct, so profound, or so pervasive."[36] America produced nearly 50 percent of the world's GDP in the late 1940s—compared with less than 25 percent today—and its military power was unmatched. Yet in 1949 America chose to create an alliance of North American and European countries and chose to run it in a democratic fashion, winning adherents by giving them a say in the alliance's decision-making structures and respecting their democratic rights.

The degree of real influence of America's Cold War allies, of course, should not be exaggerated. The Western part of the Cold War world was clearly dominated by the United States, on which the allies depended for their security, and the "equality" of allies in institutions such as NATO was only nominal. But as Princeton University scholar John Ikenberry has pointed out, instead of taking advantage of that dependence and running its alliance based on sheer power, Washington relied on "multilateralism, alliance partnership, strategic restraint, and institutional and rule-based relationships" in order to run an alliance that did not feel like an empire to its willing members.[37]

Again, the principles behind the creation of this sort of liberal order go back to the decisions made during the Truman administration. Between 1945 and 1950, faced with a nuclear-armed Soviet Union and communist aggression on the Korean peninsula, a U.S. president might have been tempted to invoke the "with us or against us" principle and rule a unilateral, pseudo-alliance. Instead, Truman gave his allies incentives to work with the United States and set up institutions designed to give them a say and a stake in the new order. Starting with the Marshall Plan, the United States demonstrated that it was prepared to subordinate parochial economic interests to shared geopolitical goals. And political, military, and economic institutions— including NATO, the International Monetary Fund, the United Nations, and the World Bank—helped to reduce suspicions of U.S. power and make Washington's leadership more palatable.

The institutions Truman set up, including NATO, reflected the democratic nature of their constituent parts. Instead of giving the United States special rights and privileges sure to generate resentment of other members, the founders of the Atlantic Alliance elaborated formal rules that asserted the sovereign equality of each of the members. America's postwar leaders understood that winning the consent of others could actually result in stronger unity and greater effectiveness than a more formal hierarchical alliance structure. According to Gaddis, "Familiarity with federalism discouraged the view that strength could override the need for negotiation and compromise. Without stopping to consider that it might have been otherwise, Truman and Eisenhower handled NATO much as they did the Congress of the United States: by cutting deals instead of imposing wills."[38]

The philosophical underpinnings behind this view of alliance management could be found in the writings of the influential Christian theologian Reinhold Niebuhr. Like other postwar "realists," Niebuhr argued that America's certainty that it was the moral side in the Cold War struggle might not be so apparent to everybody else. Americans were "not immune," he wrote, "to the temptation of believing that the universal validity of what we held in trust justified our use of power to establish it." Moreover, "a too confident sense of justice always leads to injustice. Insofar as men and nations are 'judges in their own case' they are bound to betray the human weakness of having a livelier sense of their own interest than of the competing interest."[39] In Truman's version of Niebuhr's argument, "We all have to recognize—no matter how great our strength—that we must deny ourselves the license to do always as we please."[40]

Truman's successor, Eisenhower, was even more sensitive to the need to lead by example, drawing on lessons learned in his long military career. "A platoon leader," he said in 1954, "doesn't get his platoon to go that way by getting up and saying, 'I am smarter, I am bigger, I am stronger, I am the leader.' He gets men to go with him because they want to do it for him, because they believe in him."[41] Eisenhower also shared Niebuhr's concern about the risk of arrogantly assuming universal appreciation for America's natural virtue. "We are [so] proud of our guarantees of freedom in thought and speech and worship," he wrote, "that, unconsciously, we are guilty of one of the greatest errors that ignorance can make—we assume that our standard of values is shared by all other humans in the world."[42] Thus Eisenhower, in contrast to Bush's "with us or with the terrorists" mantra, believed that the United States should not punish potentially neutral countries in the Cold War but instead give them reason to want to side with Washington. "I want to wage the cold war in a militant, but reasonable, style," he said in 1957, "whereby we appeal to the people of the world as a better group to hang with than the Communists. I am not concerned in buying friends or purchasing satellites or any other thing—that is all false. As a free country, the only ally we can have is a free ally, one that wants to be with us—that is what we are trying to develop."[43]

The United States, of course, did not always abide by this enlightened view of alliance management, and its allies often saw their powerful partner as a bully. In the 1956 Suez Crisis, the Eisenhower administration forced Britain and France to abandon their military intervention in Egypt by waging a form of economic warfare against them on the currency markets. This perceived betrayal in turn encouraged France to develop its independent nuclear deterrent, and in 1966 France withdrew from NATO's unified military command structure. In Vietnam, the United States insisted that it was fighting communism in the interest of the West as a whole and put pressure on its allies to support its cause, as it did again when it provided logistical support to Israel in the 1973 Yom Kippur War. In 1981, Washington threatened sanctions against key European allies over their support for a gas pipeline with the Soviet Union, and a few years later it pressured the Europeans to stick by their commitments to deploy American Pershing II and cruise missiles in a test of alliance solidarity.

But even when such crises occurred, they still demonstrated NATO's essentially democratic nature and confirmed the differences between the alliance and the Soviet-led Warsaw Pact. When France asked the Americans to leave French territory in 1966, some of President Johnson's hard-line advisers called for retaliation, but Johnson took a more confident, respectful view of alliance management. "When a man asks you to leave," he remarked, "you take your hat and go."[44] Over Vietnam and the Middle East crises during the Nixon years, Henry Kissinger privately railed against Europe's "craven" and "contemptible" policies, but the Nixon administration ultimately respected their sovereign decisions and worked to find pragmatic ways to overcome differences and maintain overall alliance unity.[45] In the Soviet gas pipeline dispute of the 1980s, Washington was forced to accept Europe's economic sovereignty. And in the 1983 crisis over the Pershing missiles, the democratic allies chose to proceed with the deployment, but no one doubts that the United States would have respected their decision had they chosen not to. Indeed, the decision to deploy the missiles in the first place came from a European request to Washington to bolster its nuclear deterrent, not from an American demand.

These various crises highlight the fractiousness of an alliance of democracies. But at the same time they demonstrate how the commitment to democratic principles and respect for differences among sovereign actors ultimately strengthened the alliance as a whole. NATO was not an alliance of true equals, but it did develop norms that included recognition of and respect for specific allies' vital interests and a commitment to consultation to ensure that there were no surprises and that all allies' views were heard. "Management by consensus," NATO historian Lawrence S. Kaplan wrote in 1988, "marked an alliance of free and surprisingly equal partners."[46] The contrast with the Warsaw Pact— governed under the "Brezhnev Doctrine" that gave Moscow the right not only to dictate the Pact's direction but even to intervene in member states as it saw fit—could not have been more stark. By the time the Cold War ended, every member of NATO wanted to remain in a U.S.-led alliance—and most members of the now dissolved Warsaw Pact wanted to join it as well.

FIGHTING THE RIGHT BATTLES

Not everything America did during the Cold War helped to shorten its duration or ensure its successful outcome. Indeed, and perhaps not surprisingly, Washington also fell prey to certain tendencies that probably lengthened the struggle, reduced its chances of success, and proved costly in terms of money and lives. One of these mistakes—which also offers lessons for today—was the tendency to see communism as one vast, monolithic movement. As George Kennan later pointed out, America demonstrated a curious tendency "to search, at all times, for a single external center of evil, to which all our troubles can be attributed, rather than to recognize that there might be multiple sources of resistance to our purposes and undertakings, and that these sources might be relatively independent of others."[47] The result was a costly failure to identify and exploit differences between nationalists and communists—and among different communists—around the world.

It was not that no one perceived the potential divisions within the communist world or recommended efforts to exploit them. Kennan himself was one of the first to do so. Based on his reading of history, he was skeptical that diverse nations and cultures could long be subsumed by an alien political movement, and he expressed confidence that Western European communists, Josip Broz Tito's Yugoslavia, and Mao Zedong's China would all want to keep their distance from Moscow. The United States should encourage and welcome such a trend, he advised, but it should do so quietly, so as not to fuel "the Soviet propaganda effort by assuming responsibility for a process of disintegration which communism had brought upon itself."[48] "There is a possibility," Kennan commented in September 1949, "that Russian Communism may someday be destroyed by its own children in the form of the rebellious Communist parties of other countries. I can think of no development in which there would be greater logic and justice."[49]

Reinhold Niebuhr also saw early on the possibility for divisions within the communist world, especially between the Soviet Union and China. As early as 1948, he wrote, "A Communist China is not as immediate a strategic threat as imagined by some. The Communism of Asia is primarily an expression of nationalism of subject peoples and impoverished nations. . . . It may take a long time to prove that we are better friends of China than Russia is. But if Russia should prove as heavy-handed in dealing with China as she has with the Eastern European nations, it may not take as long as it now seems."[50]

Similar points were made by State Department and CIA analysts around the same time. "Moscow faces a considerable task in seeking to bring the Chinese Communists under its complete control," one official analysis concluded in late 1948.[51] But convincing American politicians that communism was not monolithic proved a more difficult task. In 1949, an analyst for the State Department's policy planning staff, Ware Adams, argued that U.S. policy had "endorsed Stalin's own thesis that all communists everywhere should be part of his monolith. By placing the United States against all communists everywhere it has tended to force them to become or remain part of the monolith, since they would otherwise be helpless outlaws between the two all-inclusive camps of communists and anti-communists." Specifically, Adams added, "in China, the communists are somewhat pressed toward being friends of the Kremlin by the fact that they can never be friends of ours." He concluded, "If we could redefine our policy toward communism in such a way as to distinguish it from Russian imperialism, we would thus remove [a] major political force binding the satellites to the Soviet Union, and in addition remove from the communists in China and elsewhere throughout the world a strong force tending to compel them to collaborate with the Soviet Union."[52]

In fact, by the mid- to late 1950s the CIA was arguing that splits within the communist world were developing and should be exploited.[53] But these arguments were rejected by those political leaders who continued to see communism as a single movement, coordinated by Moscow, with a design to take over the world.

This was certainly the view put forward by top U.S. officials at the time. In 1954, Secretary of State John Foster Dulles publicly defined international communism as a "vast monolithic system which, despite its power, believes that it cannot survive except as it succeeds in progressively destroying human freedom."[54] Dulles often told visitors that all one had to do to anticipate communist behavior was to read Stalin's *Problems of Leninism,* "the present-day Communist bible . . . [that] gives us the same preview Hitler gave in *Mein Kampf.*"[55] Around the same time, Undersecretary of State Walter Bedell Smith called communism "a movement to bring all of the people in the world under one all-powerful central authority," and Dulles's brother, CIA Director Allen Dulles, said the communist conspiracy had "its headquarters in Moscow, an affiliated organization in [Beijing], and branch offices in Warsaw, Prague, and many other centers."[56]

This view of the enemy was hard to refute—by definition no one could prove that Moscow was not secretly coordinating all the world's anti-American movements, and no one could demonstrate in advance that it might be possible to wean some of them away from Moscow's orbit. But if the assumption of a monolith was plausible and politically convenient, it was also erroneous. Mao's China was certainly communist, but it was hardly a natural ally of the Soviet Union—as the Sino-Soviet split and America's outreach to China under Richard Nixon and his successors later proved. In Vietnam, Ho Chi Minh's struggle—begun in 1945 against the French—was at least as nationalist as it was communist, and Vietnam's 1979 war with China was certainly not the act of a communist pawn. In the Middle East and Latin America, various regimes and leaders adopted left-wing economic policies and had all sorts of historical grievances against the United States, but that hardly made them unwavering members of a global communist alliance.

"Had Washington been more attentive to the differences within international communism," the political analyst Fareed Zakaria has pointed out, "the Sino-Soviet split might have taken place earlier, Egypt might have defected from the Soviet camp earlier and, perhaps most important, the rift between Beijing and Hanoi might have developed earlier, changing completely the character of the Vietnam

War."[57] By failing to appreciate the degree to which governments in these and other places had their own, distinct interests, American policy helped to turn the notion of a communist monolith into a self-fulfilling prophecy.

★ ★ ★

Given the differences between the Cold War and the challenges America faces today, one could never hope to derive specific policy guidelines from the former, only general principles. But the general principles that proved so successful during that long struggle remain relevant today. By learning to manage the threats it faced, preserving the values of its society, showing faith in its own ideology, and winning over friends and allies around the world, the United States managed to prevail over an adversary that for years—decades, even—seemed nearly invincible. Washington inevitably made mistakes. U.S. society was not always a model for others, civil liberties were sometimes abused in the name of national security, America was often perceived by allies as a bully, and Americans tended to conflate a diverse array of threats into a single one, missing opportunities to exploit differences and leading to costly interventions like Vietnam. On the whole, however, none of the great fears—domestic or foreign—of the early Cold War period were realized, and the outcome, after more than four decades, was peaceful and nearly total victory. That should be the goal today as well, and reaching it will require developing specific policies that emerge from the Cold War's broader lessons.

3 ★ THE RIGHT WAR

It is not too late to start fighting the right war. But doing so will require a change of mind-set and a change of leadership. In its second term the Bush administration has curbed some of the excesses of the first, and it can still make some useful adjustments. But the president, the vice president, and much of their core team have shown themselves to be too invested in their long-standing conceptions to make the necessary changes—and they are now too distrusted at home and abroad for those changes to have the desired effect.

The defenders of George W. Bush's policies regularly insist there is no realistic alternative to them. Secretary of State Condoleezza Rice has asserted, "This president has a program for the war on terror and it's a program that is going to win"; adding, "I frankly haven't heard an alternative posed for how we fight the war on terror except on the offense."[1] The author and columnist Robert Kagan also considers Bush's policy as an almost inevitably "American" approach, determined primarily by the country's historical penchant for fighting moral wars and by its tremendous relative power. Kagan argues that even a Democratic victory in the

2008 election would not significantly change U.S. foreign policy, for the Democrats do not offer, in his view, "an alternative doctrine."[2]

It is certainly true—as Kagan has eloquently argued in two recent books—that American foreign policy has shown broad continuity over the country's history, but it is not true that there was no serious alternative to the set of policies Bush adopted in 2001, or that there is no serious alternative to that approach today.[3] One of the great tragedies of the post-9/11 era is that President Bush did not use the unprecedented political capital he gained in the wake of the terrorist attacks to build broad domestic and international coalitions for policies that would deny the terrorists' aims, undercut their message of hatred, and demonstrate the attractiveness of the American system. Bush could have taken bold steps on energy policy, on fiscal policy, on public and military service, and on diplomacy in the greater Middle East. Like his Cold War predecessors, Bush could have emphasized the importance of maintaining a strong, free, and appealing national society, even during wartime. Had he done so, the American public and much of the world would have rallied to his side. But he did not. Instead, Bush declared the wrong war, and the consequences are all too apparent.

To reverse these trends, America urgently needs a new framework for thinking about and pursuing a strategy to defeat Islamic extremism. Much like the strategy that won the Cold War, the new policy must consist of efforts to maintain the long-term strength and appeal of American society, prevent enemy attacks, encourage alternative hopes and dreams for those tempted by extremism, and bolster America's international legitimacy and support. Instead of taking on the impossible task of trying to kill or capture all the terrorists, we must understand that they will only be defeated when their ideology is defeated and their strategy has failed. And we should be confident that with the right set of policies, that is exactly what will happen.

RESTORING MORAL AUTHORITY

The first priority in developing a new approach to the fight against terrorism is to restore America's squandered moral authority. From the start, the administration and its supporters have downplayed the consequences of actions like the invasion of Iraq and the practices and abuses at places like Guantánamo and Abu Ghraib. The United States was attacked on 9/11, this argument goes, and thus it had the right and duty to take whatever action it deemed necessary to prevent future attacks. President Bush and his defenders have presumed that American decency was as obvious to the rest of the world as it was to them, and that nothing in particular had to be done to demonstrate it. In contrast to Dwight Eisenhower, who even in the face of the Soviet menace warned about not "destroying what we are attempting to defend," and former secretary of state Colin Powell, who now worries that the world is beginning to "doubt the moral basis for our fight against terrorism," Bush and his supporters seem to believe that the threat we now face makes such concerns irrelevant.[4] In the words of John Yoo, the former Justice Department legal adviser who wrote many of the legal memos on torture and detainee treatment, "What president would put America's image in the United Nations above the protection of innocent civilian lives?"[5]

The problem, however, is that "America's image" is in many ways what this fight is all about. It is not a question of simply being liked by others, or even doing the right thing, but of pursuing national self-interest by not providing fodder for those who are prepared to resort to violence because of America's "image." It is true that core al Qaeda members or other committed terrorists are unlikely to be mollified by a U.S. commitment to implement the Geneva Conventions. But it is also true that in a political war of ideas, millions of people around the world are judging U.S. actions to determine whether they want to be on America's side, fight against it, or sit on the fence. There is no doubt that Muslim anger over Iraq or the treatment of detainees is sometimes manufactured, manipulated, and exaggerated, but there is also no doubt that some U.S. actions have intensified genuine feelings of antipathy—even violent hatred—of the United States in a wide swath of the world's Muslim population. When pictures and stories from Abu Ghraib, Guantánamo, and Iraq circulate on jihadist Web sites, they serve as gifts to al Qaeda recruiters who are fighting a propaganda war against the United States. America needs to fight and win that war, too, and must not deny that it is taking place or inadvertently work for the other side.

The case for a careful approach to prisoner treatment— and implicitly the case against the administration's track record—is made persuasively in the new U.S. Army counterinsurgency manual, which states: "Any human rights abuses or legal violations committed by U.S. forces quickly become known throughout the local populace and eventually around the world." The manual's authors also note that these abuses "undermine both long-term and short-term [counterinsurgency] efforts." The manual points out that detainee abuse also directly fuels popular support for the enemy, because most of the people picked up in sweeps are likely to be innocent and are ultimately released back into the population. "Security forces that abuse civilians," the manual states, "do not win the populace's trust and confidence [and] may even be a cause of the insurgency."[6] These "lessons" are not new. In fact, they were identified more than forty years ago in David Galula's classic book *Counterinsurgency Warfare: Theory and Practice,* which drew on the author's experience with the French army in Algeria. Galula argued that the most effective way to demoralize enemy forces was not through abuse or torture, but rather "by employing a policy of leniency toward prisoners." Over the long run, he argued, lenient treatment saps the anger of the insurgents and makes it harder for them to bring in new recruits.[7]

The question of America's "image" is also important when it comes to winning allied support for the fight against terrorism. Indispensable allies like Afghan president Hamid Karzai, Pakistani president Pervez Musharraf, Jordanian King Abdullah, and Turkish prime minister Recep Tayyip Erdogan are severely undermined when they have to explain to their people why they should work closely with a country that has a documented reputation for abusing Muslim prisoners. Similarly, when parliaments in Britain, Spain, Italy, South Korea, Australia, or Japan vote on whether to send troops to Afghanistan, allow base access for U.S. forces, vote with the United States at the UN, or expand intelligence cooperation, they inevitably take into account their public's perception of America's "image." It is indisputable that our moral authority is being questioned, even by our closest allies. In the words of *The Economist,* the traditionally pro-American British publication, "The claim that America is free to do whatever it wishes with the Guantánamo prisoners is unworthy of a nation which has cherished the rule of law from its very birth, and represents a more extreme approach than it has taken even during periods of all-out war. It has alienated many other governments at a time when the effort to defeat terrorism requires more international cooperation in law enforcement than ever before."[8]

What can the United States do to restore its damaged reputation? There are no quick fixes, but a new administration could take steps that would go a long way. One would be to close the Guantánamo prison and finally prosecute, transfer, deport, or release (and continue to monitor) its remaining prisoners. Taking such an action would not be without risk, for the released prisoners might commit terrorist acts, as some of them have reportedly threatened to do. But on balance, the advantages of removing this stain on America's reputation outweigh the risks. After five years in isolation in a U.S. prison, the remaining detainees are unlikely to possess any significant intelligence value. Moreover, the most clearly dangerous among the prisoners can be tried by military commissions and, if found guilty, sentenced to long and legitimate prison terms. Others could be transferred to prisons in the United States, where they would at least come under the authority of a legal system that has not lost credibility as Guantánamo has. And the rest could be sent back to their home countries and tracked by U.S. or other intelligence services. That tracking would doubtless be imperfect, but as some of the detainees reestablish old contacts it might also produce new intelligence leads. And though the idea of releasing even one person who might turn to terrorism is certainly abhorrent, the sad reality is that there seems to be no shortage of willing, angry, and resentful young Muslim men to serve as operatives for international extremist groups. Indeed, continuing to hold prisoners at Guantánamo probably creates more potential terrorists than releasing those that remain.

Thinking more creatively, as it released the prisoners the United States could also orchestrate leaks that some of them had "turned" while in prison and were now working with the United States. It would be left to al Qaeda to try to figure out whether this was true (as in some cases it might well be), thus augmenting suspicion within its own ranks. Such tactics have been used successfully before—for example, by Mao Zedong's forces in the Chinese civil war. According to David Galula, who was once a captive of the Chinese communists, Mao's forces treated their nationalist prisoners well and tried to recruit them before giving them the option of returning to their units. The released prisoners were viewed with suspicion by their former associates, and some eventually sought to change sides.[9]

Another essential step will be for the United States to restore its reputation by declaring a new policy on the Geneva Conventions and torture. The next president should announce that the Geneva Conventions will be applied to all detainees and that no detained suspect will be held incommunicado without periodic visits from the International Committee of the Red Cross. To give credibility to these measures, this policy would officially rescind George W. Bush's "signing statement" appended to the McCain Amendment, in which

Bush effectively said that as president he did not feel obliged to follow the amendment's provisions. While abiding by the Geneva Conventions, the United States should also launch an international effort to clarify what rules should govern the detention of prisoners captured in a nontraditional conflict such as the war with al Qaeda, as proposed by the 9/11 Commission.[10]

Critics may argue that this would mean sacrificing what Bush calls the "tools" our interrogators need to extract intelligence, but as John McCain has observed, "Subjecting prisoners to abuse leads to bad intelligence, because under torture a detainee will tell his interrogator anything to make the pain stop."[11] Whereas Bush has asserted that "alternative procedures" used at secret CIA prisons produced valuable intelligence from prisoners like Osama bin Laden's former associate Abu Zubaydah, others, including Zubaydah's CIA interrogator, have challenged such claims, calling Zubaydah relatively unimportant and highly unreliable.[12] The issue of coercive interrogation is obviously and necessarily murky, but a recent study by the Intelligence Science Board concluded that there is little solid proof that such measures work, and good reason to believe that they can produce inaccurate or false information.[13]

Finally, a new administration must commit to a policy of transparency to reassure Americans and non-Americans alike that the era of secret prisons, warrantless wiretaps, and secret financial monitoring programs is over. Transparency does not mean that the United States will cease to engage in covert or intelligence activities vital to the nation's security, but that it acknowledges and publicly defends the need for those activities. The type of actions the United

States is undertaking will be revealed, but the details will not be.

Senator Lindsey Graham noted in August 2005 that "we should always remember that we are Americans, possessing values superior to those of our enemy. . . . This value system is our national strength, not a weakness. . . . We will win this war by showcasing the differences between the United States and the enemy."[14] In other words, just as Kennan said almost sixty years earlier, the greatest danger would be to "become like those with whom we are coping."

RETHINKING HOMELAND DEFENSE

In the long run, victory in the struggle against terrorism will come only when potential terrorists realize that extremist Islamism is a bankrupt ideology and turn to other means and ends. But that does not mean that nothing can be done in the meantime to make America safer. Indeed, the reality that there is no quick fix to the terrorism problem makes it imperative to develop the strongest preventive and defensive mechanisms possible while pursuing broader strategies to cope with the more fundamental sources of the problem.

During the Cold War, playing defense meant maintaining credible nuclear deterrence and deploying NATO troops to contain the Soviet Union while waiting for the day when the Soviet system would collapse of its own weight. Today defense has a somewhat but not entirely different meaning. States and organizations can still be deterred—not many leaders who might be tempted to give sanctuary to an Islamist terrorist group will be keen to suffer the fate of the Taliban and its leadership after 9/11. Syria and Iran may be real problems, but their leaders, who value power more than ideology or geopolitical goals, know that crossing certain lines would mean the end of their regimes, and probably the end of their lives. For non-state groups such as al Qaeda, whose operatives (but not necessarily their leaders) are prepared to die, deterrence does not work. In that case, playing defense means doing everything possible to deny the terrorists the possibility of achieving their primary goal, to create terror. The next administration will need to prioritize among potential targets, improve capacity to thwart attacks in advance through improved intelligence and international cooperation, provide the public with a more realistic assessment of the terrorist risk, and above all, avoid exacerbating the problem by allowing terrorists to provoke us into counterproductive actions.

Since 9/11, significant efforts have been made to better protect the United States from terrorist attacks. The defense-policy experts Kurt Campbell and Michael O'Hanlon have pointed out that since 2002 homeland security spending has increased by at least 300 percent to more than $40 billion per year; airline cockpit doors have been hardened; more passenger luggage is being screened; thousands of armed air marshals have been deployed; millions of doses of antibiotics and smallpox vaccine have been stockpiled; and containers coming into U.S. ports are now two to three times more likely to be screened than prior to 9/11.[15] It is impossible to know whether any of these measures have helped prevent any actual attacks, but it is probably safe to conclude that it is harder for terrorists to strike certain targets—notably airplanes, a long-standing preferred target for al Qaeda—than it was prior to 9/11.

That said, these kinds of defensive measures are limited in two fundamental ways. The first is that such activities are mostly designed to prevent a type of attack that has already occurred—and is therefore unlikely to be repeated. Efforts to prevent airline passengers from taking command of planes and flying them into buildings, for example, would have been extremely useful in 2001, but are probably not pertinent today, now that passengers are much more alert to the possibility of such a threat. Second, and even more important, there are far too many potential targets in the United States. As Campbell and O'Hanlon point out, the United States contains more than half a million bridges, nearly five hundred skyscrapers, nearly 200,000 miles of natural gas pipelines, more than 2,800 power plants, and countless schools, theaters, restaurants, subway systems, and shopping malls.[16] To try to protect all of them would be prohibitively expensive, and to protect some but not others would only displace the threat from one site to another. Even if somehow the resources were found to "harden" all of these targets we would still be immensely vulnerable. In the fall of 2002, after all, the population of Washington, D.C., was terrorized for weeks by an "organization" that consisted of a homeless Gulf War veteran and a fifteen-year-old boy operating with one rifle and a 1990 Chevrolet Caprice. The two snipers managed to kill more than a dozen people and were stopped only when they tried to extort $10 million from the government.[17]

Politically, it is hard to argue against any type of defensive measure, and no elected leader wants to be the one who voted against an initiative that might have prevented an attack on his or her watch. But since not every potential target can be protected, the priority for defensive homeland security measures needs to be placed on stopping those attacks that would have catastrophic "spillover" effects on the rest of society or the economy.[18] Though a shooting or a bombing anywhere would obviously be horrific, the United States must put particular emphasis on preventing attacks that would cause massive loss of life and destruction or that would shut down large sectors of the economy. These include attacks on nuclear and chemical plants, airports and seaports, and any attacks with nuclear or biological weapons. Instead of devoting precious resources to the impossible task of protecting everything, the United States should focus on expanding international programs to examine cargo in foreign ports and to interdict vessels carrying potential weapons of mass destruction, developing better nuclear tracking and screening technologies, and stockpiling more effective antidotes to biological weapons while improving networks for their rapid delivery to potential victims.[19] New technologies that can help prevent catastrophic attacks include explosive-sniffing machines in airports, iris identification scanners and other biometric technologies, "smart containers" with tamper-proof seals and transponders, and systems to counter the threat to civilian aircraft from surface-to-air missiles. These technologies are all expensive. But considering that the Bush administration's tax cuts for Americans earning over $1 million per year amount to more than $47 billion for 2007 alone—a figure greater than the entire 2007 budget for the Department of Homeland Security—they are hardly unaffordable.[20]

Even more important than protective measures are improvements in our capacity to identify and thwart attacks in advance through better intelligence. Although some progress has been made since 9/11, there is room for improvement. Because the FBI, with its long-standing focus on traditional law enforcement and criminal prosecution, has proven incapable of undertaking the required domestic intelligence tasks, the United States should establish a domestic intelligence agency outside the FBI, along the lines of Britain's MI5 or the Canadian Security Intelligence Service. Although a good case can be made that such a major reorganization would be too complicated and too distracting for a system of intelligence and law enforcement that has already undertaken major recent reform, a new administration should at a minimum undertake a study of how such a service could be created in time. The advantage of a separate agency for domestic intelligence is that its dedicated career agents would be trained to focus on anticipating future attacks, infiltrating terrorist groups, and getting necessary intelligence to the law enforcement officers who need it, rather than, like the FBI, gathering case information after the fact and jealously guarding it lest a legal process be compromised.[21] Other necessary measures include breaking down barriers to information sharing among different government agencies and the military, ensuring that the legal process to protect civil liberties does not unduly impede domestic information-gathering activities like wiretapping, and training far more intelligence officers in languages like Arabic, Urdu, Farsi, and Hindi so that critical audio intercepts and foreign documents can be translated in a timely and effective manner.[22]

Preventive measures can be highly effective in helping to dismantle terrorist networks and plots. Every single one of the fourteen "high-value terrorists" the United States is now holding at Guantánamo, for example, was captured not on a battlefield but by foreign intelligence services or foreign and U.S. services working closely together. This list includes Khalid Sheikh Mohammed, the 9/11 mastermind who was captured in Pakistan in 2002; Abu Zubaydah, a bin Laden associate captured in Pakistan in 2002; Abd al-Rahim al-Nashiri, an al Qaeda operations chief captured in the United Arab Emirates in 2002; Ramzi bin-al Shibh, a 9/11 coordinator captured in Pakistan in 2003; Hambali, the operational leader of the Indonesian extremist group Jemaah Islamiyah, who was captured in Thailand in 2003; Lillie, a Hambali lieutenant captured in Thailand in 2003; and Abu Faraj al-Libi, an al Qaeda communications conduit captured in Pakistan in 2005. Preventive measures based on intelligence have also succeeded in foiling a number of serious plots, including what may have been the most serious terrorist threat since 9/11, the alleged plan by dozens of British Muslims to blow up airliners, a plan that was thwarted by MI5 in the summer of 2006.[23]

Of course, Bush administration officials often point out that even preventive efforts have their limits, because, as President Bush has noted, "the terrorists have to be right only once to kill our people, while we have to be right every time to stop them."[24] This mantra is true, but it does not necessarily follow that more aggressive policies or military operations are well advised. Indeed, though it is certainly frustrating to accept that not every terrorist attack can be prevented, there is a good case for a homeland security version of the Hippocratic Oath: "First, do no harm." Although there will certainly be times when military force is necessary, there will be at least as many times when either preemption or overreaction would be counterproductive. As the Australian counterinsurgency expert David Kilcullen has put it, "It is not the people al-Qaeda might kill that is the threat. Our *reaction* is what can cause the damage. It's al-Qaeda plus our response that creates the existential danger."[25]

The United States must remember that the terrorists' primary goal is not death and destruction for its own sake, but rather the public terror that their attacks are designed to provoke. Therefore, instead of overstating an allegedly "existential threat," the country's leaders would be better served by putting the threat in perspective and reassuring Americans how relatively safe they actually are. Political scientist John Mueller has pointed out that even including the 3,000 deaths from the 9/11 attacks, the number of Americans who have died from international terrorism since the State Department began counting in the 1960s "is about the same as the number killed over the same period by lightning, or by accident-causing deer, or by severe allergic reactions to peanuts."[26] Put another way, by the terrorism expert Brian Jenkins of the RAND Corporation, "The average American has about a 1 in 9,000 chance of dying in an automobile accident and about a 1 in 18,000 chance of being murdered. During the past five years, including the death toll from 9/11, an average American has had only a 1 in 500,000 chance of being killed in a terrorist attack." If the years 1997 to 2006 are taken into account, "the probability of dying at the hands of terrorists drops to 1 in a million."[27]

It is of course safer for politicians to play up the terrorist threat than to risk appearing to ignore it, but overstating and overreacting to the threat only helps terrorists accomplish their goals. Our leaders should take the opposite approach: do everything reasonably possible to prevent terrorist attacks—especially catastrophic ones—from occurring, but also put the threat in perspective and refuse to allow terrorists to sow fear. Allowing an alienated and angry teenage Muslim to believe he can affect the foreign and military policy of the most powerful country in the world can be a powerful incentive to undertake an act that would give meaning to his life. Treating such acts with contempt—and demonstrating that they are futile and irrelevant—would help to deter them.

PROVIDING HOPES AND DREAMS

Playing better defense is only a temporary, imperfect fix. Defensive measures must be combined with a long-term strategy to address the sources of the problem. Part of the agenda for doing so involves Middle Eastern diplomacy in Iraq, Iran, Israel, Afghanistan, and elsewhere, which is the focus of the next chapter. But fighting and winning the right war also means doing more to provide hope and a sense of dignity to angry, alienated, humiliated Muslims who risk turning to terrorism to give meaning to their lives. Living in a part of the world that has fallen behind nearly all others in terms of economic and social development and has seen the successive failures of colonialism, secular nationalism, and socialism, they need reasons to believe in a compelling dream that is not utopian Islamist extremism. A Middle East in which human rights and freedoms are respected, jobs are plentiful, and income is more evenly distributed would be a

Middle East less likely to see some of its citizens tempted by the call to extremism.

During the Cold War, the most important mechanism in undermining the enemy ideology was the demonstration effect. Over time it became manifestly clear that capitalist societies aligned with the United States were freer, richer, safer, and less corrupt than the communist ones they were aligned against. All anyone had to do was travel from West Berlin to East Berlin—or even to observe the difference on television—to see who was winning the Cold War and to give those living under communism the inspiration to change.

The United States and its allies actively reinforced this demonstration effect with other measures designed to promote the sort of economic and social development that would inoculate populations from the temptation of communism and to win hearts and minds around the world. These included Truman's "Point Four" program, which provided technical assistance to and encouraged private investment in developing countries, Eisenhower's creation of the United States Information Agency, which sponsored exchange programs, English-language courses, and American cultural events; Kennedy's Alliance for Progress, designed to help provide homes, health, work, and schools for underprivileged Latin Americans; and Kennedy's Peace Corps, which sent tens of thousands of enthusiastic young American volunteers all over the world to promote economic development and cultural understanding and to improve the image of the United States. The United States also set up American Cultural Centers, which housed libraries and provided forums for American speakers and performers and broad-casting agencies such as Radio Free Europe/Radio Liberty and the Voice of America, which provided an alternative to communist propaganda or state-run news agencies in the Third World. Until their budgets were slashed at the end of the Cold War, these and other efforts helped to alleviate poverty, provide education and information, and promote the image of the United States around the world.[28]

To its credit, the Bush administration has identified the problem of the lack of hope and freedom in the Muslim world. But it has not done enough; it has confused democracy with liberalism and the rule of law, and it has under-mined its own efforts with policies that so tarnished the image of the United States that America's help is often no longer welcome. The administration at times oversold its agenda—for example, with Bush announcing the utopian goal of an "end of tyranny" in his 2005 State of the Union speech—and it was also too quick to claim success that same year when elections in Iraq and Afghanistan, public protests in Lebanon, and tentative steps toward open elec-tions in Egypt and Saudi Arabia gave the false impression that democracy was already "on the march." Rather than put-ting misplaced hope in the idea that the United States can install democracy through regime change, what is needed now is a new team of actors without the Bush administra-tion's baggage, an expansion of efforts to promote change and create hope, and the determination and patience to help Muslim societies evolve in a more open direction.

One aspect of the administration's approach that needs to change is its tendency to equate "democracy" with elec-tions and to see democracy as a realistic or even desirable near-term goal in the Arab world. This is not to say that Arabs are incapable of democracy but rather to note that societies deeply divided along sectarian, tribal, and religious lines (and which have had little or no experience with the rule of law and constitutions) risk exploding if elections are organized before the necessary conditions for stable democracy are in place. The risk is not only that at present Islamists would win free elections in just about every Arab state, but that most elections would produce "tyrannies of the majority" that could be just as bad as the undemocratic tyrannies they would replace.[29]

Instead of pushing regimes to start with elections, the focus of U.S. policy should be bringing about the conditions in which democracy could ultimately be created and sustained by the Arabs themselves. Such conditions include more balanced economic development; better education and higher literacy rates; development of the rule of law and functioning justice systems; respect for human rights and freedom of speech; empowerment of women; and a reduction in corruption. Progress in these areas would make democracy more plausible down the road and would do much to give citizens of the region reasons to have pride in the accomplishments of their culture. Job creation, education, and opportunities for women would help slow the demographic explosion that is leading to a potentially dangerous "youth bulge." Such changes would also give more young people reason to stay and work at home, rather than to emigrate to places like Europe, where the difficulty of social integration has become part of the problem.

To help promote these goals, the Bush administration has taken some useful first steps. These include the Middle

East Partnership Initiative, which seeks to promote free-market economic reform, political freedom, education, and women's rights; the Broader Middle East and North Africa Initiative, which seeks to promote political dialogue, entrepreneurship, microfinance, literacy, and democracy; and a proposal for a Middle East Free Trade Area, designed to build on bilateral free trade agreements and culminate in free trade among Middle Eastern states and with the United States by 2013.[30] These kinds of initiatives need to be expanded, better funded, and complemented with other efforts. One would think that a country that spends around $375 million per day in Iraq could find the resources necessary to promote education, social and political change, and economic development in such an unstable and important region.[31] Indeed, consider this: just *one week's* worth of spending on the Iraq war (around $2.6 billion during 2007) would be enough to fund the entire budget of the Middle East Partnership Initiative (around $100 million); the entire public diplomacy budget for the Muslim world ($150 million); an expansion of the Peace Corps by some 10,000 volunteers (around $400 million); the opening of a new American cultural center in every Arab capital ($400 million); and scholarships to American universities for 10,000 students from the Middle East ($400 million), with over a billion dollars left to spare.

The United States must also offer more economic and diplomatic incentives to countries that make progress toward the program's goals. America already provides some $5.5 billion in economic and military assistance to the Arab world, beyond what it is spending in Iraq. It may be impractical to withhold much of that aid from countries like Egypt underdevelopment and violent extremism. The failure to create rewarding jobs leaves many young Muslims with nothing to do or hope for; huge income inequality resulting from oil revenues that accrue only to elites breeds resentment of ruling ethnic groups or royal families; the lack of adequate resources in poor states deprives their governments of the capacity to monitor and fight terrorism even when they want to; and overall economic backwardness is a source of shame for members of a once-great culture that has been left behind.[33] Many scholars have also shown the strong linkage that exists between balanced economic development and the spread and sustainability of democracy. Indeed, other than the rich Middle Eastern states, whose income distribution is skewed by oil revenues, all countries with a per capita income level above $6,000 have developed into democracies. And the causality runs from prosperity to democracy rather than the other way around: the growth in income helps the emergence of an educated and independent middle class with an interest in the rule of law, a more open society, and the opportunity to influence and limit the power of governments through free and fair elections.[34]

For all these reasons, the United States needs to see economic engagement and development as an essential tool in its confrontation with terrorism. A new secretary of state in 2009 would do well to put his or her name to a major new program for Middle Eastern economic development in the same way that Secretary of State George Marshall did in 1947, when the Marshall Plan brought hope to so many Europeans. This new plan would not have to provide the same level of aid as the Marshall Plan—a level that the region in any case probably could not absorb and the U.S. Congress is probably not ready to provide—but it does mean pushing for the same sort of open markets and economic cooperation among Middle Eastern states that the Marshall Plan helped promote in Europe during the early years of the Cold War. Indeed, the new administration should do more than endorse the Bush administration's goal of a Middle Eastern free trade zone by 2013; it should unilaterally and immediately offer increased duty-free access to certain Arab-produced goods. Economist Edward Gresser has pointed out that reaching free trade agreements with Central America, the Andes, and Africa but not the Middle East may be good for the participants but it actually puts Middle Eastern goods at a relative disadvantage—which only further contributes to unemployment, political tension, and support for extremists.[35] To provide jobs and give hope to people in key Muslim states like Pakistan, Egypt, and Turkey, the United States should be seeking to promote their exports, not displace them.

Promoting good governance and providing economic opportunities to Muslim countries are thus worthy goals, and it is essential that we expand our efforts to reach them. We will never manage to promote either democracy or more balanced economic development in the Middle East, however, until we accomplish an ambitious economic and social goal of our own: weaning ourselves off the region's oil.

ENDING THE OIL CURSE

America's excessive reliance on imported Middle Eastern oil has become a prominent political issue for a number of reasons. In 2006, the price of a barrel of oil shot up to an unprecedented $70 per barrel, leading to gasoline prices averaging above $3 per gallon and causing great public discontent. Also in 2006, the scientific consensus that human activity was having a potentially catastrophic effect on the global climate became almost impossible to ignore, leading even the once-skeptical Bush administration to warn the country about an "addiction to oil" and to call for a reduction in the use of oil and gasoline.[36] The implications of high oil prices for American foreign policy have also become clear. With oil nearly three times as expensive as it was in the mid-1990s, Washington has little leverage on countries like Russia, Iran, Venezuela, and Sudan as they throw their new weight around in international politics and as the international community shows reluctance to confront them.

American dependence on imported oil is not only bad for Americans, however. It is bad for the oil exporters themselves—and strongly contributes to the lack of democracy and widespread popular resentment that fuel the terrorism problem. Countless studies have shown the relationship between economies that live off exports of a single natural resource and the tendency toward undemocratic rule.[37] It is not a coincidence that nearly all of the world's main oil exporters—including Saudi Arabia, Russia, Iran, Iraq, Venezuela, Kuwait, and Nigeria—are authoritarian regimes. (Of the world's top fourteen petroleum exporters, only Norway is a liberal democracy.) The luxury—or curse—of being able to rely exclusively on a single, valuable export dug out of the ground leads to huge income disparities, enables autocratic governments to buy off the public instead of undertaking difficult reforms, dispenses citizens from having to learn skills or crafts, and drives up the exchange rate, making exports of other goods relatively less viable. Countries such as Japan, South Korea, Taiwan, and Singapore—without significant natural resources of their own to export—have had to develop and succeed in the world through hard work, education, and broad-based economic development. Countries like Saudi Arabia, Iran, and the Gulf States have not felt the need to do so. The result is a group of some of the most repressive countries in the world, from whose populations a significant proportion of Muslim terrorists have come.

In addition to fostering autocracies, our failure to move decisively away from dependence on oil and the subsequent high oil prices that failure produces means, as *New York Times* columnist Thomas Friedman has argued, that we are effectively "funding both sides in the war on terror."[38] With cash flowing in from high oil prices, countries like Saudi Arabia can use some of the extra dollars we spend on imported oil to promote radical strains of Islam and co-opt violent extremists, and countries like Iran can finance terrorist groups like Hezbollah. Even Qatar, a Persian Gulf state friendly to the United States, donates $50 million out of its oil and gas revenues to Hamas.

The often overlooked role played by rising and falling oil prices in ending the Cold War is relevant here. The energy crisis of the 1970s—when oil prices quadrupled in 1974 and more than doubled again in 1979—was a boon to the oil-rich Soviet Union. The price rise kept the Soviet economy afloat, allowed the government to subsidize weak sectors like defense and agriculture, and gave Moscow the confidence to challenge the weakened West geopolitically, in Central America, Africa, and Afghanistan. Beginning in or Pakistan that violate practices of good governance, since it could actually make the situation worse. But Washington should be prepared to provide additional aid to countries like Jordan and Morocco that govern increasingly well, as an incentive to them and to others. Helping good performers show tangible benefits could have a positive "spillover" effect in the region.

Initiatives like these can give Arab regimes the incentive to undertake the types of reforms that will improve their societies, promote justice, provide hope for their citizens, and bolster national pride and honor, thus helping to diminish the frustration and despair that contributes to extremism. But economic engagement with the Middle East can also contribute by providing jobs, growth, and more balanced economic development, which itself can serve to undermine extremism. Poverty itself, as numerous scholars have pointed out, is not a direct cause of terrorism. The vast majority of terrorist attacks over the past decade have been planned or carried out by middle-class Muslims like the 9/11 ringleader Mohammad Atta, a graduate student in architecture from a wealthy Cairo suburb; or Ayman al-Zawahiri, the deputy head of al Qaeda who is a medical doctor, not to mention the fabulously wealthy Osama bin Laden.[32] If poverty were the primary cause of terrorism, moreover, Haiti, Niger, and Madagascar would be among the world's leading producers of terrorism, which they are obviously not. Al Qaeda leaders, in all their pronouncements, rarely raise the issue of economic injustice and focus instead on geopolitical injustice, foreign occupation, and cultural humiliation.

But there are clear indirect links between economic

the mid-1980s the United States launched a deliberate strategy to drive down oil prices, with the goal of undermining the Soviet economy. According to Ronald Reagan's national security adviser Richard Allen, this effort was led by CIA Director William Casey, who persuaded Saudi Arabia to increase production from two million to nine million barrels per day. The oil price consequently fell from over $30 per barrel to $12 per barrel, cutting Soviet revenues by some $10 billion per year.[39] After coming to power in 1985, Mikhail Gorbachev could no longer buy off key domestic constituencies or subsidize Soviet allies in Eastern Europe or elsewhere, and he soon had to give up in the geopolitical competition with the West. He realized that only major domestic reform, economic modernization, and peace could save his country. Today, so long as oil prices remain at current levels, none of the Middle Eastern autocracies needs to make that choice.[40]

For all these reasons, it should be an urgent national priority to begin to reduce our dependence on foreign oil—as indeed it should have been in the wake of 9/11, when the American public was likely to embrace such a policy in the name of confronting the terrorist threat. Bush's call in January 2007 to increase the use of alternative fuels, raise fuel economy standards for cars and trucks, and reduce gasoline use by 20 percent over the next ten years is thus welcome, but it is far too little too late. The support for alternative fuels is constructive, but the "goal" of reducing gasoline usage is nothing more than the sort of vague aspiration that presidents have been proclaiming regularly—and failing to reach—since the oil crises of the 1970s.

New technologies currently under development have the

potential to help reduce American oil dependence.[41] One of the most promising is the development of "plug-in hybrid vehicles," designed to run on a combination of gasoline and electricity. The up-front costs of such vehicles is relatively high (around $5,000 to $6,000 more than conventional vehicles), but because their batteries can be charged at night when electricity demand is low, their potential for significantly reducing oil use is considerable. According to the Brookings Institution's David Sandalow, plug-in hybrids could replace one-third of the oil in U.S. light-duty vehicles by 2025. Similarly, increased use of "biofuels"—ethanol produced from corn or sugar, or eventually from cellulosic sources such as switchgrass, corn stalks, or fast-growing trees—can help reduce U.S. oil demand. Continued tax incentives for ethanol use, and the removal of the 54 cent tariff on imported ethanol (which helps keep cheap sugar-based ethanol from Brazil out of the U.S. market), could further contribute to a reduction in oil demand.

A genuinely serious U.S. policy to end its "oil addiction" would include an increase in the federal gasoline tax to discourage consumption and to encourage consumers to purchase more energy-efficient vehicles. Though it would require political courage to propose a significant increase, the benefits would be significant. The federal tax has remained at just 18.4 cents per gallon since 1993 (when President Bill Clinton raised it by 5 cents as part of a deficit-reduction plan). Increasing the gasoline tax by one dollar per gallon, for example (which would still leave U.S. gas prices far lower than they are in Europe), would raise over $100 billion per year, reduce the use of gasoline by between 3 and 6 percent from its otherwise expected growth path, and spur the purchase of fuel-efficient cars. The combination of these effects could end up reducing long-run use of gasoline by about 16 percent.[42] Even a more politically palatable increase in the gas tax of 20 cents per gallon would still raise close to $28 billion, which would be enough to give $6,000 tax credits to one million purchasers of plug-in hybrids—or to set aside for spending on education, health care, homeland security, the environment, tax cuts, or other purposes that might have political constituencies of their own.[43] And the argument that the higher energy prices that would result from these policies would damage the economy is hard to sustain. From 2004 to 2006, oil and gas prices rose by more than 30 percent—and the increases were accompanied by strong economic growth.

A creative alternative to raising the gas tax would be to take the opportunity created by higher oil prices to ask Congress to impose a "price floor" on a barrel of oil. Under such a mechanism, the government would announce that, as part of a comprehensive energy strategy, it would henceforth not allow the price of oil to fall below a particular floor of, say, $60 per barrel. If high oil prices continued, the proposal would have little impact and cost nothing, either politically or financially. But if prices fell below that level—as they might well do once the impact of recent prices on demand and investment in alternative energy sources work their way through the world economy—the government would intervene to keep the price stable, with the difference between the floor and the market price reverting to the state as revenue.

If consumers and industry knew that the price of a barrel of oil would never again fall below $60 per barrel (the level around which U.S.-produced corn-based ethanol fuel becomes economically viable), they could make long-term investment and consumption decisions in a way that makes little economic sense so long as price stability is not guaranteed. Americans will not make long-term decisions to buy fuel-efficient automobiles, create distribution networks for alternative fuels, or invest in technologies like hydrogen fuel cells, flex-fuel vehicles, or wind power unless they know that a future sharp fall in oil prices will not undercut them.

Many would argue that a price floor on oil or even a modest increase in the gas tax, however it is packaged politically, is impossible. That view, however, overlooks the way in which public attitudes are changing as Americans begin to realize the national security and environmental implications of relying so heavily on imported oil. A poll in February 2006 found that 85 percent of Americans still said they opposed a gasoline tax, but when asked whether they would support such a tax if it reduced the United States' dependence on foreign oil, 55 percent of respondents said they would.[44] If leaders clearly explained what was at stake, the American public could be persuaded to make a small sacrifice in the name of national security.

With much of the increase in the global demand for oil coming not from the United States but from emerging economies like China and India, the United States cannot solve this problem alone. Still, even at just 4.6 percent of the world's population, America consumes some 25 percent of the world's oil. Its role in shaping global demand, in persuading other countries to move away from oil dependence, and in developing the technologies that would allow them to do so, is considerable. As the country most responsible for bolstering the market for Middle Eastern oil—and the country most susceptible to the negative economic, environmental, and security consequences of that market—the United States should become an example to the rest of the world by leading the global effort to end the oil curse.

REBUILDING FRAYED ALLIANCES

Fortunately, much of what the United States needs to do to have more success in defeating the terrorist threat is in Americans' own hands. But the United States cannot win this war alone. Just as winning the Cold War required constant efforts to maintain the support of allies, defeating terrorism will require significant international cooperation— for intelligence sharing, joint judicial and police work, multilateral sanctions and incentives, and military operations. An America that is popular, respected, reliable, and admired has a far better chance of winning needed cooperation in these areas than an America that is not.

The second-term Bush administration seemed to recognize this point. Indeed, starting in January 2005, it appeared to realize it had paid a price for gratuitously alienating allies and that diplomatic efforts to repair relations were worthwhile. Secretary of State Rice stated in her confirmation hearings that "the time for diplomacy is now" and immediately set off on a fence-mending trip to Europe, where the costs of U.S. unilateralism had become most apparent. A few weeks later, the president himself went to Europe, where he reached out to allies in a way that sharply contrasted with the unilateralism and "divide and rule" approach of his first term. The new tone and style was also reflected in the foreign policy team Bush and Rice put together, as many prominent conservatives (such as Paul Wolfowitz and Douglas Feith) left the administration, others were moved out of policymaking jobs (John Bolton), and pragmatic professionals (including Robert Zoellick, Philip Zelikow, Nicholas Burns, and Christopher Hill) came on board.[45] Bush also modified a number of internationally unpopular policies: he agreed to support European diplomatic efforts on Iran and even to offer potential U.S. "incentives," he stopped his aggressive opposition to the International Criminal Court, and he gave new priority to multilateral negotiations with North Korea over its nuclear program. Bush had hardly become a committed multilateralist and he was still deeply unpopular abroad, but at least he seemed to be acknowledging that the United States needed more international support, and that such support was not automatic.

A new administration will have to go much further if it is genuinely to restore America's frayed alliance system. Having a new face in the White House will itself do much to restore many allies' disinclination to work closely with the United States. So, too, would the adoption of some of the policies advocated above—on detainees and energy use, for example. While no one should expect the United States and its allies to see eye-to-eye on all the world's difficult challenges, a new president who closed Guantánamo, unambiguously ruled out torture, agreed to cooperate with the International Criminal Court, and took serious steps to combat global warming would immediately benefit from a huge dose of international goodwill.

The new leader must also restore the leadership style that served Truman, Eisenhower, Kennedy, and other presidents so well during the Cold War—one not based simply on power and determination but also on the willingness to show respect for and listen to allied points of view. At one point, even George W. Bush understood this. As a presidential candidate in 2000, he wisely noted: "It really depends upon how our nation conducts itself in foreign policy. If we're an arrogant nation, they'll resent us. If we're a humble nation, but strong, they'll welcome us. And . . . our nation stands alone right now in the world in terms of power, and that's why we have to be humble."[46] Bush may not have followed his own advice, but it will behoove a future president to heed these words, as Eisenhower, Truman, and other Cold War presidents did even when faced with great challenges.

Restoring relations with allies would not only help the United States combat terrorism by strengthening cooperation in key areas like intelligence, law enforcement, homeland security, and military operations. It would also make it easier to leverage the rest of the world's money, troops, and diplomatic influence as we confront the enormous but inescapable challenge of dealing with the geopolitical disaster that is the greater Middle East.

4 ★ A NEW DEAL FOR
THE MIDDLE EAST

The Cold War was a global war, but its key battleground was in Europe. The challenge there was not just to deter a potential Soviet invasion, which the United States did with the deployment of more than 300,000 troops and the extension of unprecedented defense guarantees to an alliance. The challenge was to persuade millions of Europeans that their security and their well-being would be best assured in close association with America, and not as part of the Soviet empire or even as neutrals. The United States won that battle unambiguously, and the European Union is now a liberal, capitalist, and democratic zone of peace encompassing some 450 million citizens.

Today's battleground—the key battleground for the war on terror—is the greater Middle East. Just as millions of Europeans had to make their choice in the 1950s, 1960s, 1970s, and 1980s, now millions of Muslims must decide whether to join the extremists, extend them support, remain neutral, or actively pursue a liberal and nonviolent future in cooperation with the United States and its allies. Just as America was not truly safe during the Cold War until all of

Europe was unambiguously on America's side and the extremist ideology that threatened it was shown to have failed, America will not be safe now until extremist Islamism suffers a similar fate.

After 9/11, the Bush administration rightly concluded that the old Western "deal" with the region's leaders—whereby they sold us oil, bought our weapons, and avoided upsetting the regional geopolitical status quo in exchange for our overlooking the way they treated their own citizens—was no longer acceptable, and President Bush set out to "transform" the region. But the Bush approach to transformation depended on flawed premises. It was based on a vast exaggeration of American power, overconfidence in international support for the United States, naive optimism about the prospects for Western-style democracy in the region, excessive confidence in the American public's patience, and an underestimation of the costs of U.S. disengagement from the Israeli-Palestinian peace process. The result is a Middle East that is even more unstable, no more democratic, and far more hostile to the United States than it was when Bush set out to transform it.

The next American president will have to adopt a new approach. It cannot be based on the failed notion that enough military power and determination will force "the enemy" to accommodate American interests and desires or that democracy is a panacea for the scourge of terrorism. A new strategy for the Middle East and for the war on terror must instead be based on some of the same principles that served us so well in the Cold War: containing threats that cannot be eliminated at acceptable cost; preserving our values to help win over adversaries' hearts and minds; building legitimacy to preserve strong alliances; and choosing battles carefully, based on both their importance and our prospects for success. No one should underestimate how difficult it will be to improve a truly catastrophic situation. But changing course now, and applying these principles, will set our Middle Eastern policy—and thereby the war on terror—on a new and more positive course.

GETTING OUT OF IRAQ

Historians—and politicians—will debate for a long time to come whether the Iraq war was a good idea badly implemented or whether the operation was doomed from the start. Either way, there is certainly a good case for the thesis that the war was badly managed. Faced with an admittedly difficult problem, the Bush administration applied worst-case analysis to the risk of inaction, but best-case analysis to the case for action—leading it to act against a threat that was not nearly as great as it claimed and leaving it poorly prepared for the predictable chaos that followed the overthrow of Saddam Hussein.

The operational mistakes and misjudgments of those who managed the war and occupation have been thoroughly documented. They included not sending enough troops to provide security in a country of 26 million people; failing to secure weapons caches and allowing looting to take place in the days and weeks following the fall of Baghdad; disbanding the Iraqi army and pursuing aggressive de-Baathification without plans for the former soldiers or Baathists (moves that left thousands of angry, humiliated, unemployed Sunnis primed for revenge); failing to understand the nature of the insurgency and the importance of winning support from the general population; and appointing inexperienced ideologues with political credentials instead of seasoned professionals to key positions in postwar Iraq.[1] Given the stakes, all of this amounted to strong evidence of serious negligence on the part of those responsible for it.

That said, it remains far from clear that the Iraq invasion would have proved successful even if the United States had done everything "right." Many initial supporters of the war still insist that the occupation could have succeeded had it only been better managed. We will never know, but the reality may be that the goal of creating a stable post-Saddam Iraq was simply unattainable. Iraq was an artificial entity held together only by brute force and ruled ruthlessly and disastrously for decades. Thus when the United States removed the country's security and administrative structures— however horrible they may have been—the result was a highly predictable internal struggle for security and resources. The conditions within Iraq—a vengeful Shiite community that had been violently oppressed for decades; Kurds who had long enjoyed de facto independence from Baghdad; sharp divisions among various ethnic groups; immensely valuable oil resources up for grabs; insecure and rapacious neighbors determined to influence Iraq's future; a strong cultural resistance to perceived colonial occupation; and the absence of a domestic leadership class, which had been eliminated or chased from the country by Saddam— were hardly conducive to stability no matter what the occupiers did. It may well be that even if the United States had sent twice as many troops and retained Saddam's army to help ensure security, it still would be facing an equally violent and chaotic Iraq—just in different ways and for different reasons.

Whichever view is right is at this point almost immaterial, though it is worth noting that those who designed the Iraq war violated almost all of the principles advocated here: they conflated diverse threats into a single one, took the risk of trying to eliminate a threat they could have lived with, overlooked the importance of legitimacy and international support, and created more enemies than they destroyed— all at enormous financial and human cost. Proponents of the war have spent much time underscoring the differences with the Vietnam War, and of course the differences are many. But what is similar is that in both cases the United States underestimated the power of nationalism, placed too much importance on maintaining "credibility," and failed to see that its actions played into the "colonialism" narrative of its ideological opponents. In both cases, demonstrating resolve, failing to distinguish between the particular battle and the broader war, and repeatedly putting false hopes in military escalation plans ended up costing thousands of lives, billions of dollars, and creating resentment all over the world. The question today is how to choose among bad options to manage a miserable situation. In the context of the war on terror, the goal must be to end an American military presence that has become a recruitment tool for al Qaeda without allowing Iraq to become the sort of failed state that would serve the terrorists' cause.

The Bush administration decided in January 2007 to increase the U.S. military presence and apply counterinsurgency tactics in Baghdad in a new effort to bring security to Iraq. The argument behind the troop surge is that providing greater security in the capital can buy time for Iraqi leaders to make progress on political negotiations that would help calm the insurgency and prevent sectarian infighting. If Iraqi leaders can reach agreements on issues like revenue sharing from oil exports, de-Baathification reform, amnesty for former insurgents, and the disarmament of militias, the argument runs, the causes of the insurgency and the incipient civil war will be vastly reduced. In addition to the "positive" case for staying in Iraq, the administration also makes a "negative" case: withdrawing U.S. troops would undercut America's allies in Iraq, increase the likelihood of all-out civil war, and, in the words of Vice President Cheney, "validate" the strategy of the terrorists.[2]

The case for maintaining U.S. troops in Iraq—or even increasing their number—is not without logic. It is true that violence could significantly increase in the wake of a U.S. military withdrawal, and also true that this would be celebrated as a victory for America's opponents. Given U.S. responsibility in producing the current situation in Iraq in the first place, no argument in favor of withdrawal should be made lightly. If maintaining large numbers of American troops in Iraq could help produce a stable democracy, the achievement of that outcome would be a defeat for the terrorists, a boon for Iraqis, and a hugely positive signal to the rest of the Middle East.

The sad reality, however, is that the addition of some 20,000 troops—an approximate 15 percent increase of the overall U.S. presence—is unlikely to be enough to bring security to Baghdad's more than five million citizens, let alone the rest of the country. More likely, regrettably, is that the parties to the Iraq conflict are now too determined to prevail over their enemies to allow for the necessary political deal, and that even a deal among elected leaders in Baghdad would not stop the battles under way. Even before the cycle of violence unleashed by the bombing of the Mosque of the Golden Dome in Samarra in February 2006, the conflict in Iraq had transformed from what was primarily an insurgency against U.S. forces—which might have been controllable with enough troops and the right strategy (America had neither)—into primarily a civil war, which is beyond America's capacity to stop. It is worth recalling that in the late 1950s and early 1960s, France deployed more than 400,000 troops to Algeria, whose population of around 10 million was less than half of Iraq's today. Yet despite the deployment of overwhelming force, ruthless repression, and absolute determination on the part of French leaders, France was unable to pacify the insurgency.

A large and increasing U.S. military presence in Iraq may well play a role in keeping the violence from getting even worse, but it is also a provocation to Iraqi nationalists on all sides and a gift to Islamist terrorists, as it appears to confirm their narrative of a Western imperialism whose goal is to occupy Arab lands. According to opinion polls taken in spring 2007, 78 percent of Iraqis (including more than 80 percent of Shiites and 97 percent of Sunnis) oppose the presence of U.S. and other forces in Iraq. More than 70 percent of Shiites and nearly all Sunnis think the presence of U.S. forces is making security worse. And 51 percent of Iraqis (94 percent of Sunnis and 35 percent of Shiites) approve of attacks on U.S.-led forces (up from 47 percent in January 2006 and 17 percent in February 2004).[3] Americans may resent that Iraqis are not more grateful for their help in removing a horrible dictator who killed hundreds of thousands of Iraqis, but that does not change the reality of Iraqi perceptions today. The stabilization of Baghdad and a new political agreement among the parties would be the best outcome in Iraq. But Americans also need to prepare for the day when it is clear to all that the costly American military presence is simply not contributing to the achievement of that goal.

When that day comes, the best course will start with a U.S. announcement of a clear date, coordinated with the full range of Iraqi political and sectarian leaders, for the planned departure of American troops. Making clear that U.S. forces are leaving Iraq would have several advantages. First, it would undercut the argument made by Iraqi nationalists and manipulated by al Qaeda that the U.S. intention is to remain as the colonial master of Iraq. It was always odd to argue—as many early proponents of the war did—that the presence of 5,000 American troops in Saudi Arabia was a major cause of terrorism but that the presence of 150,000 Americans in Iraq would not be.[4] President Bush argues that if America were to withdraw from Iraq "the enemy" would emerge with "new safe havens and new recruits and new resources and an even greater determination to harm America."[5] In fact, the opposite might be the case: ending the perceived American occupation of Iraq could undercut the motivation of terrorists and their sponsors and allow Iraqis to focus on their difficult enough national struggles.

Second, the withdrawal of U.S. combat forces from Iraq would send a message to the Shiite-controlled government in Baghdad that it can no longer count on the U.S. military to fight its battles for them. Until now, that government has been able to count on up to 150,000 U.S. troops that have essentially been helping it try to suppress Sunni insurgents. Though American forces are theoretically opposed to all armed groups not under the control of the government, they have not been willing to confront the large and well-armed Shiite militias, nor do they have the capacity to do so without provoking more violence, producing more civilian casualties, and increasing the chances of conflict with Iran. The prospect or reality of a U.S. withdrawal could also help persuade rebellious Sunnis to seek a political settlement in Iraq by eliminating their fantasies that Washington would restrain the Shiite majority and help Sunnis regain their lost dominance of Iraq.

Finally, withdrawing from Iraq would limit what has been a hugely costly diversion of American finances and manpower from other tasks. Given America's lack of success in building a stable and democratic Iraq, it is hard to argue that the more than $400 billion and 150,000 troops that have been deployed there would not be better spent on other aspects of the war on terror—from bolstering our effort in Afghanistan to creating jobs and providing education in the Middle East or decreasing our reliance on imported oil.

Setting a date for the withdrawal of U.S. armed forces from Iraq would not mean simply leaving the country to its fate. If during a phased U.S. withdrawal the Iraqi government started to make progress on containing the violence or reaching political agreement, the timing and pace of the withdrawal could be reconsidered. The United States could also use the period in between the setting of a withdrawal date and actual departure to help the parties in Iraq negotiate a Bosnia-like federal agreement along the lines of that proposed by Senator Joseph Biden and former Council on

Foreign Relations President Leslie Gelb.[6] Even after a withdrawal, the United States could maintain significant forces in the region (in Kuwait and the other Gulf states) to deter Iraq's neighbors from overt military intervention, train Iraqi security and police forces, and potentially conduct raids against al Qaeda leaders or camps that might be in Iraq. The United States could also continue to provide economic and political support for Iraq's government and help train the judges, lawyers, civil administrators, utilities managers, and other officials it will need to succeed.

The United States cannot extricate itself from the Iraq quagmire without damage or risk. But stubbornly pursuing a failing course—at a heavy cost in terms of American lives, resources, and reputation, all while failing to prevent insurgency and civil war—is not the answer, either. Whatever the damage may be to U.S. credibility and in the war on terror, the reality is that staying in Iraq is already damaging America's prospects, and to a greater degree and at a higher cost. The same was true in Vietnam. As George Kennan told the Senate Foreign Relations Committee in 1966, "There is more respect to be won in the opinion of this world by a resolute and courageous liquidation of unsound positions than by the most stubborn pursuit of extravagant and unpromising objectives."[7] Fighting the war in Vietnam for another six years (at the cost of tens of thousands more American lives and further deterioration in U.S. standing in the world) did not help us win the Cold War any more than perpetuating our position in Iraq today will help win this one. Indeed, though leaving Vietnam in 1975 entailed real and significant short-term costs both for the Vietnamese and the United States, in the longer run it helped to stabilize America's global position, enhanced its reputation around the world, and helped it win the Cold War. In 2006, President Bush visited an increasingly prosperous and democratizing Vietnam that had embraced capitalism and sought good relations, and free trade, with the United States.

PURSUING ISRAELI-ARAB DÉTENTE

Another top priority for the Middle East must be for the United States to reestablish itself as an honest broker between Arabs and Israelis and to make far more energetic efforts to bring about an Israeli-Palestinian peace. This is necessary not only for the sake of Israelis, Palestinians, and the countries on their borders, but also because achieving genuine peace in the region would be an enormous contribution to America's efforts in the war on terror. Any U.S. administration that delivered an Israeli-Palestinian peace not only would strongly undercut the arguments of Islamic extremists but would also earn considerable credibility and goodwill in the Muslim world and across the globe.

The Bush administration and its supporters have always downplayed the link between Islamist extremism and Middle East peace. They point out, rightly, that many Arabs cynically manipulate the Palestinian issue—bin Laden uses it as a means of rallying support for his cause, and many Arab dictators invoke it to shield themselves from criticism of their own failings. It is true that al Qaeda has many grievances with the West beyond the Palestinian issue and that the 9/11 attacks were conceived and planned during a period when the Clinton administration was actively pursuing an Arab-Israel peace. Yet just because terrorists and extremists exploit the

Palestinian issue does not mean that it is not an issue. Indeed, opportunism is possible only where real anger and emo-
tion create an opportunity to exploit. And that is the case with
the Palestinian issue today.

There is in fact a significant body of evidence indicating
that the Palestinian tragedy has contributed to the thirst for
revenge and quest for honor that is behind the modern Islamist terrorist movement. Israel's very foundation was the
initial humiliation, as the relatively small number of Jewish
immigrants to Palestine managed to destroy a coalition of
Arab armies and set up the Jewish state. But as journalist
Lawrence Wright shows in *The Looming Tower,* his study of
al Qaeda's origins, it was the 1967 Six-Day War that led
many Arabs to turn away from the region's failed nationalist
movements and to look instead for salvation to a radical
brand of Islam. The 1967 war was the "psychological turning point in the history of the modern Middle East," according to Wright. "The speed and decisiveness of the Israeli
victory . . . humiliated many Muslims who had believed
until then that God favored their cause. . . . The profound
appeal of Islamic fundamentalism in Egypt and elsewhere
was born in this shocking debacle."[8]

Wright and others have also shown how the Palestinian
issue has long influenced the thinking of members of al
Qaeda. When bin Laden was thirteen years old, according
to his mother, he "experienced a religious and political
awakening. . . . Sometimes he would sit in front of the television and weep over the news from Palestine." As a teenager,
"he was the same nice kid, but he was more concerned, sad,
and frustrated about the situation in Palestine in particular,
and the Arab and Muslim world in general."[9] Bin Laden

himself dates his hatred for the United States—and even his idea of attacking the World Trade Center—to 1982, when "the idea came to me when things went just too far with the American-Israeli alliance's oppression and atrocities against our people in Palestine and Lebanon. The events that made a direct impression on me were during and after 1982, when America allowed the Israelis to invade Lebanon with the help of its third fleet [sic]. . . . As I looked at those destroyed towers in Lebanon it occurred to me to punish the oppressors in kind by destroying towers in America, so that it would have a taste of its own medicine and would be prevented from killing our women and children."[10]

Almost a generation later, the same factors would influence the lead hijacker of the 9/11 attacks, Mohammad Atta. According to Wright, "On April 11, 1996, when Atta was twenty-seven years old, he signed a standardized will he got from the al-Quds mosque. It was the day Israel attacked Lebanon in Operation Grapes of Wrath. According to one of his friends, Atta was enraged, and by filling out his last testament during the attack he was offering his life in response."[11]

For extremists like bin Laden and Atta, even a comprehensive Israeli-Palestinian peace would not be enough—bin Laden warned not long after 9/11 that "America will not live in peace before peace reigns in Palestine, and before all the army of infidels depart the land of Muhammad," which may be a long time in coming.[12] But for many Muslims around the world who may be tempted to join, support, or sympathize with al Qaeda or similar groups, the issue of Israel and its relationship with its neighbors is critical. And pretending that it is irrelevant in the war on terror is a critical mistake.

Unfortunately, Bush came into office more determined to avoid getting bogged down in Israeli-Palestinian negotiations than to try to make such negotiations succeed, and he has remained unwilling to engage fully in the issue ever since. His reluctance stemmed from his perception of Bill Clinton's failed efforts. For seven years following the 1993 Oslo agreement, the Clinton administration made achieving a Palestinian-Israeli peace settlement a top priority, devoting huge amounts of energy, time, money, and political capital over the course of the president's two terms in office, culminating in the Camp David Summit in 2000. The failure to achieve an agreement at Camp David was an object lesson to Bush. In his view, Clinton had pushed the Israelis to offer more than they ever had before in the name of peace, and had even put forward proposals that may have exceeded what Israeli domestic politics would accept—and still the response from the Palestinian side was terrorist violence, supported by Palestinian leader Yasser Arafat. Bush concluded from this experience that deep engagement was not worth the effort or the risk of failure, so he withdrew. He refused to deal with Arafat, formed a close partnership with the hawkish Israeli prime minister Ariel Sharon, and did not press either of his two secretaries of state—Colin Powell or Condoleezza Rice—to intervene more than episodically in the region.

Bush had a different theory of how Middle East peace would come about—through demonstration of resolve and the democratic transformation of the region. In contrast to Clinton's attempt to "contain" both Iraq and Iran while working on Israeli-Arab peace, Bush chose the opposite approach: he put Israeli-Arab peace on hold in order to focus on Iraq and Iran. As Bush explained it in early 2003, "Success in Iraq could . . . begin a new stage for Middle Eastern peace, and set in motion progress toward a truly democratic Palestinian state. The passing of Saddam Hussein's regime will deprive terrorist networks of a wealthy patron that pays for terrorist training and offers rewards to families of suicide bombers. And other regimes will be given a clear warning that support for terror will not be tolerated. Without this outside support for terrorism, Palestinians who are working for reform and long for democracy will be in a better position to choose new leaders."[13] In other words, according to a widely used formulation at the time, the road to Baghdad would not pass through Jerusalem, but the road to Jerusalem would pass through Baghdad.[14]

Sadly, things have not worked out as Bush expected. Resolve, diplomatic disengagement, and regime change in Iraq were followed not by Palestinian compromise or capitulation but rather by years of terrorism, violence, the absence of a peace process, and, in January 2006, the election of the extremist Islamist group Hamas to a majority in the Palestinian parliament. The Clinton approach may not have produced peace, but the opposite of the Clinton approach did not seem to be succeeding either.

In early 2007, the Bush administration appeared to have come around to the view that diplomatic engagement was necessary after all. Finally acknowledging the reality that regime change in Iraq was not going to have the hoped-for spillover effect, and under mounting pressure from European and Arab allies to act, Secretary of State Rice in January 2007 announced that she would travel to the region in an effort to restart the diplomatic process. She told Palestinian

Authority President Mahmoud Abbas that she "heard loud and clear the call for deeper American engagement" and began speaking about offering a "political horizon" for the Palestinians—a phrase the Palestinians themselves had begun to use to refer to the prospect of a final status settlement.[15] The United States would continue to refuse to deal with Hamas so long as it refused to renounce violence and recognize Israel, but Rice engaged directly with Abbas, hoping to demonstrate to Palestinians that more could be gained through moderation than through violence.

Rice even appeared to be motivated at least in part by the notion that U.S. diplomatic engagement on the Israel-Palestine issue would have wider benefits for the war on terror. Indeed, a few months earlier one of her closest advisers at the State Department, Philip Zelikow, gave a speech in which he stressed the importance of engagement on Arab-Israeli issues as a means to "bind together" a coalition of the United States, Europe, Israel, and the moderate Arab states. In Zelikow's words, "For the Arab moderates and for the Europeans, some sense of progress and momentum on the Arab-Israeli dispute is just a *sine qua non* for their ability to cooperate actively with the United States on a lot of other things that we care about. We can rail against that belief . . . but it's a fact. That means an active policy on the Arab-Israeli dispute is an essential ingredient to forging a coalition that deals with the most dangerous problems."[16] Given Zelikow's close relationship with Rice, the speech seemed to point in the direction of a new U.S. willingness to seriously address the issue. The limits of that new willingness, however, soon became apparent: the State Department distanced itself from Zelikow's remarks, no other government official endorsed the argument, and Zelikow left the government a few months later.[17]

If the United States really wants to help Israelis and Palestinians, undercut the terrorists, restore its reputation as an honest broker, and contribute to a stronger global coalition against terrorism, it will need to go well beyond Rice's tentative forays into peacemaking. The best approach would be for Washington—together with the European Union and supportive Arab states—finally to come forward with its own detailed and comprehensive plan for peace, showing precisely what each of the parties would get if they accepted it. The basics of what such an agreement would look like have been known for years, but putting it forward formally with the promise of international endorsement, financial and military backing, and solid Arab political cover would make it more likely that the parties would accept it.

The United States should propose the creation and recognition of a Palestinian state along the borders of June 4, 1967, modified through land swaps to allow incorporation of major Israeli settlement blocs into Israel; full Israeli withdrawal of settlements and military forces from the territory of the new Palestinian state; a deal on Jerusalem that would allow Israelis to govern the currently Jewish parts of the city and Palestinians to govern the Arab parts; the recognition of East Jerusalem as the capital of the new Palestinian state; a security agreement that would allow the Palestinian state to maintain a strong domestic security force but not an army; a settlement of the Palestinian refugee problem that would allow refugees to return to the new Palestinian state but not to Israel and the creation of an international compensation fund for loss or damage of property;

the deployment of a multinational force to help provide security to Israel and the Palestinian state; and acceptance by all parties, codified in a UN resolution, that Israel and Palestine are legitimate and recognized states and that the Israeli-Arab conflict was over.[18] An agreement along these lines, all of its backers would make clear to the parties, would give the Palestinians sovereignty, territory, a home for refugees, a capital in Jerusalem, and unprecedented economic opportunities, and it would give Israel security, a home within Israel for a large majority of settlers, a capital in Jerusalem, and normalized relations with most of the Arab world.

Even for a determined American administration focused on the issue, achieving such a peace will be difficult, to say the least. Part of the Palestinian Authority's government, Hamas, refuses even to recognize Israel's legitimacy, let alone negotiate peace with it, and the other half, under President Abbas, is apparently willing to do so but not able. On the Israeli side there are also huge obstacles. The Israeli public's support for unilateral withdrawal from the West Bank has been undermined by the experiences in southern Lebanon and Gaza, where withdrawal led not to peace as its proponents promised but to further attacks from Hezbollah and Hamas. The Israeli government, moreover, is almost as weak as the Palestinian Authority—if Ariel Sharon had difficulty removing 8,000 settlers from Gaza in 2005, one can only imagine how hard it would be for a prime minister without Sharon's security credentials forcibly to evacuate tens of thousands from the West Bank.

Yet even against high odds there is a strong case for at least trying to achieve peace and some reasons to believe that it is not impossible. One new factor is the renewed interest in the subject shown by some of the region's Sunni governments, now deeply concerned about the rise of Shiite power backed by Iran. When Clinton tried to make peace in 2000 these Sunni governments were not willing to press Arafat or give him political cover, but now they realize that if they do not find a way to change the current dynamic, Iran will step into the breach, as it already has done with its support for Hamas and Hezbollah in Lebanon. This fear of Iranian and Shiite influence helps explain why Saudi Arabia took the initiative to facilitate the Hamas-Fatah power-sharing agreement of February 8, 2007, negotiated in the holy city of Mecca. It also explains the new activity around the potential revival of a previous Saudi-led peace initiative, the "Abdullah Plan" of 2002. The plan—named for the then Saudi Crown Prince and now King Abdullah, who proposed it—offered full normalization between Arab states and Israel in exchange for Israeli withdrawal to the June 4, 1967, borders, a "just" resolution of the Palestinian refugee problem, and the recognition of a Palestinian state. The plan was endorsed by twenty-two Arab states at an Arab League summit in Beirut in March 2002, but neither the Bush administration nor the Israeli government at the time aggressively followed up on the proposal. Nonetheless, it would be a good starting point for the negotiations so badly needed today.[19] For five years the plan sat dormant, until the Saudis revived it and it was unanimously endorsed at an Arab League summit in Riyadh in late March 2007. The United States should seize the moment and match the Arab plan with one of its own.

Another hopeful factor is that majorities in both Israel

and Palestine still support a peace deal based on a two-state solution. Israelis are disillusioned with the results of unilateral withdrawal, but 60 percent of them still support talks with Abbas on a final status settlement, and 76 percent want to see further disengagements from the West Bank negotiated with the Palestinian Authority.[20] A majority of Israelis—58 percent—even favor direct talks with Hamas leaders if the organization frees the Israeli soldier captured near Gaza in June 2006, Gilat Shalit.[21] On the Palestinian side, when asked about their attitude toward a possible peace agreement with Israel that would establish a Palestinian state within the 1967 borders, 23 percent of Palestinians said they were "prepared to accept" this, 38 percent said they were "prepared to accept it but thought it unlikely," and only 29 percent said they were "unprepared to accept it." In other words, even if many Palestinians doubt that Israel would accept such a deal, a sizable majority say they are prepared to do so. Potential support for the difficult compromises that both sides would have to make is narrow, but it exists.[22]

Opponents of such a peace process argue that engaging with a Palestinian coalition government prior to Hamas's recognition of Israel would legitimize Hamas. But in fact, the opposite is more likely to be the case. Hamas derives its legitimacy from the perception that it is fighting foreign occupation, and the longer the stalemate goes on, the more support it gets. Putting a serious peace offer on the table would force Hamas to accept it or undermine its legitimacy by refusing the peace that most Palestinians want. And though Hamas refuses to recognize Israel today, it is not hard to imagine an eventual change in that position—as occurred with the Palestine Liberation Organization twenty years ago. In its February 2007 power-sharing deal with Fatah, Hamas leaders continued to refuse to recognize Israel, but they agreed to "respect" past agreements—including all the past peace accords with Israel. They have also stated their willingness to deal with Israel on a day-to-day basis, accepted the possibility of a long-term and renewable "truce" (*hudna*) with Israel, and made clear that future leaders and generations will decide themselves whether to go further than that.[23] Even Khaled Meshal, head of Hamas's Political Committee and one of its most hard-line officials, has publicly accepted Israel's reality. "There will remain a state called Israel, this is a fact," he has said. "The problem is not that there is an entity called Israel, the problem is that a Palestinian state does not exist."[24]

A Palestinian state that does exist would be good for Palestinians, who have waited too long to have one. It would also be good for Israel, if it is part of a general agreement that would enable it finally to live in security. And it would seriously undercut the arguments of those who seek to exploit the suffering of Palestinians in their all too successful effort to recruit terrorists willing to kill and die.

CONTAINING—AND ENGAGING—IRAN

The right war requires a new U.S. policy toward Iran. That policy should consist of renewed determination to make Iran pay a price for actions that put international security at risk along with equal determination to engage seriously with Iran and hold out the possibility of future cooperation. In other words, Iran today is a good target for the type of "long-term, patient but firm and vigilant" containment policies that proved successful against the Soviet Union. Iran's leaders are ideological, defensive, and hostile toward the United States, but its people are frustrated with a failing economy, constraints on personal freedom, and the country's isolation. In the long run, the United States must count on the Iranian people—or a bold new Iranian leader—to choose the path of constructive cooperation. But it can only do that if it puts a genuine prospect for positive relations on the table, respects Iran's legitimate interests, gives Iranians the incentive to choose a different path, and prevents its current leaders from doing too much damage in the meantime.

The Bush administration's initial approach was to focus almost exclusively on isolating Iran. In January 2002, President Bush denounced Iran as a member of the "axis of evil," and his top officials argued that engaging it would only legitimize an illegitimate regime. Instead, the administration's logic ran, the United States would demonstrate its power in Iraq, send a clear message that dictators would pay a price for their policies, encircle Iran with pro-American regimes in Iraq and Afghanistan, and oblige Iran to deal on Washington's terms.

For a short period after the fall of Baghdad in spring 2003, such an approach seemed promising. With the United States having toppled Saddam Hussein and with 150,000 U.S. troops on Iran's border, concerned Iranian leaders reached out to Washington to explore the possibility of better relations, an olive branch that was ignored or dismissed out of hand by the ultraconfident Bush administration.[25] Although apparently approved by most senior authorities in Tehran, the Iranian initiative might well have amounted to nothing, but it was consistent with past Iranian practices of demonstrating total inflexibility when playing a strong hand and compromising when playing a weak hand, and Iran's hand at the time seemed weak. Under pressure from the European Union, this relatively weak Iran had also agreed to suspend its uranium enrichment program and reprocessing activities and to enter into diplomatic talks about better economic and diplomatic relations.

Since 2003, however, the situation has reversed almost entirely. America's "victory" in Iraq turned into a costly quagmire, pro-Iranian Shiite parties have taken control of the Iraqi government, Iran's cautious president Mohammad Khatami was replaced by the hard-line radical Mahmoud Ahmadinejad, and a huge and unexpected rise in oil prices has provided a considerable cash windfall to the regime.[26] Buoyed by this sudden infusion of money and confidence while the United States was bogged down, Iran resumed its nuclear program, shrugged off the threat of economic sanctions, and expanded its flow of money and arms to groups like Hezbollah, Hamas, and the Shiite parties and militias in Iraq. Far from feeling isolated and searching for compromise, the Iranian government now feels it has the wind in its sails.

This newly confident Iran poses many threats to U.S. interests, including its aggressive pursuit of a suspected nuclear weapons program, its support to Hezbollah and Hamas, and its opposition to peace negotiations between Israel and its neighbors. It is worth noting, however, that these threats are distinct from the threat posed by al Qaeda and the terrorists who attacked the United States on 9/11. Indeed, Iran is itself an enemy of al Qaeda and shares an interest with the United States in defeating the Taliban elements that once harbored al Qaeda in Afghanistan. The Iranian challenge needs to be dealt with, but seeing it as part of a single war on terror would be as big a mistake as was fighting against an alleged communist monolith in the 1950s. Better to take measures to counter the regime's deleterious actions, increase the strains on Iranian society, and hold out serious prospects for more positive relations if there is change in Tehran.

Those who see Iran as a part of "the enemy" argue that the threat it poses is so grave that the United States should be prepared to use military force—or covert sponsorship of violence against the regime—to thwart it.[27] The Bush administration does not call for war with Iran and limits itself to reiterating that "all options remain on the table." Bush has, however, bolstered the threat of U.S. military action against Iran by deploying an aircraft carrier to the Persian Gulf in the context of the Iranian threat, accused Iran of fomenting insurgency in Iraq and supplying advanced weaponry to be used against U.S. troops there, authorized U.S. military personnel in Iraq to use deadly force against Iranian agents operating there, and insisted flatly that the United States will not allow Iran to develop nuclear weapons.[28]

If Iran continues to develop its nuclear program and increases its support to groups like Hezbollah and Hamas, the logic of the Bush single war on terror would seem to require preemptively attacking Iran. Doing so, however, would be as misguided now as it would have been to try to preempt the development of Soviet or Chinese nuclear forces in the 1940s or 1960s. Targeted U.S. air strikes probably could destroy many of Iran's critical nuclear facilities and set back the program a number of years. But U.S. intelligence about Iran is far from perfect, and even the known elements of the Iranian program are dispersed at multiple sites around the country, protected by extensive air defenses, often located near civilian areas, and sometimes buried under thirty feet of dirt and reinforced concrete. Air strikes against the nuclear program, therefore, would not be "surgical" but rather widespread, sustained, and likely to kill a large number of Iranian civilians. Even more important, a military attack would also have the probable consequence of generating strong public support within Iran for an otherwise unpopular regime—the population would then become absolutely determined to develop a nuclear weapons program, possibly even overtly.[29]

Moreover, Iran would be certain to retaliate. Through its Shiite partners in Iraq and Afghanistan, Iran could wreak havoc on U.S. forces and undermine our efforts to stabilize both countries. It could threaten oil shipments through the Strait of Hormuz and urge terrorist clients—including Hezbollah and Hamas—to launch retaliatory strikes against America and its allies. Seeking to change the regime in Tehran by aiding anti-government exile forces or other "freedom fighters" could have even more severe consequences: they would most likely fail to change the regime, give it an excuse for repression in the meantime, and even if the effort "succeeded" the result would more likely be a chaotic failed state than a pro-Western democracy. In other words, just as attacking Iraq turned a real but separate foreign policy problem into a central part of the war on terror, attacking Iran would run the risk of doing the same thing, on an even larger scale.

These bad military options underscore why a dual-track policy of containment and engagement is best for the United States and its allies, and why both elements of that policy need to be strengthened. The containment element is already well under way—and working better than many people realize. Beyond the unilateral U.S. sanctions that have been in place for years, the United States has been working closely with other countries, notably the European Union, to make Iran pay an ever-higher price for its lack of cooperation on the nuclear issue. On July 31, 2006, the United Nations Security Council surprised Iran by passing Resolution 1696 (with support of fourteen of its fifteen members, including all five permanent members), demanding that Iran "suspend all enrichment-related and reprocessing activities, including research and development, to be verified by the IAEA [International Atomic Energy Agency]." Though the resolution imposed no direct penalties on Iran, it expressed the intention to impose such penalties if Iran did not comply by August 31, and it had the advantage of making Iranian uranium enrichment illegal, which was not previously the case.[30] Two further UN Security Council resolutions, 1737 in December 2006 and 1747 in March 2007, denounced Iran's continued lack of compliance, put constraints on Iranian arms exports, and imposed limited sanctions on nuclear trade with Iran and financial dealings with people involved in the Iranian nuclear and missile programs.[31] It also held out the prospect of further sanctions if Iranian defiance continued. Russia and China remain reluctant to sacrifice their own economic and energy interests in Iran by imposing more far-reaching measures, but the fact that they have joined all the other members of the Security Council in passing resolutions against Iran has gotten the attention of many Iranians.

New U.S. financial sanctions against Iranian banks are also starting to have some effect. The U.S. Treasury Department—now authorized by the UN Security Council Resolutions—is putting pressure on European and Japanese banks not to cooperate with Iranian financial institutions linked to the nuclear or missile program, and the United States is pushing Europeans to cut government-backed loan guarantees, which amounted to some $18 billion in 2005. Along with threats of secondary U.S. sanctions against European oil companies, the result of these measures has been a significant constraint on badly needed foreign investment in Iran's energy sector. Iran is now struggling to maintain production at current levels of around four million barrels per day and some Iranian oil officials and other experts believe that with stagnant production and rising demand, Iran will have no oil left to export within a decade.[32] Such fears have led the government to consider hugely unpopular measures to ration gasoline or to lower the subsidies that make it so cheap (around 35 cents a gallon) for Iranian consumers.

There have also been signs of what one Tehran-based journalist has called "mounting public unease and the seeds of mutiny in parliament over the combative nature of [Iran's] nuclear diplomacy."[33] In the December 2006 elections for local government, most seats went to reformers and moderate conservatives, in what many observers in Iran and elsewhere saw as a rebuke against President Ahmadinejad.[34] The following month, two prominent Iranian newspapers, including one owned by Ayatollah Ali Khamenei, Iran's supreme leader, rebuked Ahmadinejad over his handling of the nuclear issue, as did Iran's most senior dissident cleric, Grand Ayatollah Hossein Ali Montazeri.[35] Montazeri said that Ahmadinejad's provocations were creating problems for the country, and, according to press reports, this "reflected a growing feeling among many that Ahmadinejad has concentrated too much on fiery, anti-U.S. speeches and not enough on the economy."[36] In an unprecedented action that same month, 150 of the 290 members of the Iranian parliament signed a letter blaming Ahmadinejad for rising inflation and unemployment and criticizing his travel to Latin America at a time when there was more pressing business at home.[37]

There is no guarantee that escalating sanctions will succeed in changing Iranian behavior or contribute to a change in the Iranian regime, but given the alternatives, it makes sense to find out. Many argue that sanctions never work, but this argument overlooks the experience in places like South Africa, Serbia, Libya, and even the former Soviet Union. During the Cold War, the prohibition of certain high-technology exports under the Coordinating Committee for Multilateral Export controls exacerbated the problems of the Soviet economy, which in turn helped produce Gorbachev and the end of the regime. When international economic and diplomatic sanctions have been broad-based, multilateral, and sustained, they have eventually had important positive effects, at least in diverse societies with educated populations, active civil society groups, and at least partially democratic institutions—like Iran.

On the engagement track, progress has also been made, but even more significant change is necessary. After years of dismissing European Union diplomacy and engagement with Iran and insisting that the United States would not "reward bad behavior," Bush in February 2005 suddenly announced, following a trip to Europe, that the United States would support the negotiations by Great Britain, France, and Germany with Iran over its nuclear program. The administration even said it would also offer its own incentives for Iranian cooperation, including the provision of badly needed U.S. spare parts for Iranian civilian aircraft (dating from the time of the Shah) and Washington's potential support for Iran's application to join the World Trade Organization. In March 2006, the administration announced its willingness to open a dialogue with Tehran about Iraq, and in May 2006 Secretary Rice said that if Iran agreed to suspend uranium enrichment, she would agree to direct multilateral talks on the Iranian nuclear program. In early 2007 Rice agreed to attend a conference hosted by the government of Iraq that would include Iranian participation.

These were all constructive steps, but Washington must go further if it truly seeks a more constructive relationship with Iran. For a start, the United States should agree to talk to Iran about any issue—and even offer to open full diplomatic relations. America maintained diplomatic relations with the Soviet Union throughout the Cold War and today it has diplomatic relations with dozens of countries that it does not particularly like—indeed, one could argue that such relations are most needed when there are contentious issues to sort out. It is hard to see what is gained from forgoing direct engagement unless one somehow thinks that the Iranians' desire to have an American ambassador in Tehran will convince them to compromise over Hezbollah or nuclear weapons.

As part of an official dialogue, Washington must make

clear to Iran that it views Iran's political future as a matter for Iranians to decide, and that it has no intention of using military force against Iran or fomenting internal dissent through the support of violent opposition groups. Given the historical record (American support for the coup that overthrew the elected Iranian government in 1953, American support for the Shah's repressive regime for decades, and American military intervention against two of Iran's neighbors within the past five years), Iran's concerns about such issues are legitimate, and official reassurance—especially from a foreign policy team without the baggage of the Bush administration—could make a difference.

Beyond that, the United States should put on the table incentives that would be available to Iran in exchange for cooperation in areas of concern to the United States. These include an end to the long-standing U.S. economic embargo, unfreezing of Iranian assets dating back to the time of the Iranian revolution, support for starting WTO negotiations, encouragement of foreign investment, technical support for a verifiably civilian nuclear program, and regional security discussions. Some of these elements—the end of sanctions, WTO negotiations, civilian nuclear support—should be on the table as part of a nuclear deal, while others—like the encouragement of foreign investment or a regional security agreement—ought to be offered as a response to progress in other areas, such as limits on Iranian support for Hezbollah or Hamas. In other words, the United States should offer not so much an unlikely "grand bargain" but rather a "gradual bargain" whereby agreements in initial areas would reduce mutual suspicion and demonstrate that areas of common interest do exist.[38]

In the end, the two pillars of this U.S. policy combined should present Iran with a long-term choice: it can become an impoverished, isolated pariah state with nuclear weapons—like the Soviet Union in its day, or North Korea now—or it can begin to reintegrate with the international community, meet the needs of its people, and preserve its security. The United States cannot make that choice for Iran, and may have to rely on a policy of deterrence and containment for many years. But it should at least be prepared to recognize Iran's legitimate interests, show the Iranian people what the alternative is, and be prepared for the day when they make a different choice.

AFGHANISTAN AND PAKISTAN

To fight and win the right war in the Middle East we need to redouble—in many areas, literally—our efforts to prevent Afghanistan from returning to the chaos that led to Taliban rule and sanctuary for al Qaeda. Afghanistan was a key battleground during the Cold War, and American efforts to turn it into the Soviet Union's Vietnam succeeded. But those efforts came at a high price: stoking Osama bin Laden's delusion that his Arab mujahideen could bring down a superpower. When the United States walked away after the Soviet defeat and left Afghanistan to its fate, the Taliban filled the vacuum and ultimately provided al Qaeda with the base from which it attacked America. This time around, we must not fail to leave the country better off than when we found it.

The Bush administration initially made admirable efforts in Afghanistan. The ouster of the Taliban in November 2001 was a tremendous success: more than four million refugees returned to their homes; Afghanistan's neighbors came together to support a political process; the most competent and legitimate government in the country's history was elected; the first national parliament in thirty years was opened; and a broad international coalition that included America's NATO allies sent aid and troops to help stabilize the country.

Over the past several years the situation in Afghanistan has taken a serious turn for the worse, however, in part because of the diversion of U.S. attention, troops, money, and specialized intelligence assets to Iraq. Pakistan's inability or unwillingness to confront the regrouping Taliban forces along the Afghan-Pakistan border has also been a big part of the problem. Combined with inadequate international military and economic support, the security and political situation is now in a parlous state. A failure to stabilize Afghanistan would be a massive setback in the effort to fight terrorism and deny al Qaeda a new base.

The main problem in Afghanistan today is the rising level of violence. The Taliban and al Qaeda, clearly inspired by the success of insurgents in Iraq, have begun copying their methods. Suicide attacks, which had previously been virtually unknown in Afghanistan, rose from 27 in 2005 to 139 in 2006, and the use of remotely detonated roadside bombs doubled during the same period from 783 to 1,677.[39] The aim of the attackers is to make the local population doubt the ability of the government to protect them, to test the staying power of NATO forces by inflicting casualties and making it necessary for more troops to be sent, and to provoke NATO into military actions that cause civilian casualties, thus undermining local support.

Such tactics have proved successful. Some NATO members (the United States, Britain, Canada, the Netherlands, Poland) have steadfastly accepted the rising challenge, though others (Germany, Italy, France) have restricted their deployments to the relatively safe northern or western parts of the country. The overall NATO rules of engagement are robust, but many allied forces also operate under so-called national caveats that limit the circumstances under which their troops can join the fight (for example, ruling out dangerous missions such as flying at night or outside restricted geographical areas). Rising allied and civilian casualties have also led some national parliaments—including those in Italy, Spain, and the Netherlands—to question seriously whether to continue to support the NATO mission.

The trends in the area of opium production—long another scourge of Afghan society—are also going in the wrong direction. Mountainous, arid, landlocked, mismanaged, and torn by violence for more than thirty years, Afghanistan is the poorest country in the world outside of sub-Saharan Africa—leading many of its farmers to turn to poppy cultivation just to feed their families, even if that means breaking the law. The 2006 opium harvest was the highest ever, and Afghanistan now furnishes over 90 percent of the global illicit opium trade.[40] By some accounts, up to 50 percent of Afghanistan's GDP is now derived from poppy cultivation. Drug trafficking is a serious threat to Afghanistan's legal economy because it empowers drug lords, funds the Taliban, and diverts other potential production into the much more lucrative opium trade.

Despite all these problems, Afghanistan is far from lost, and the Afghan public remains relatively positive about both the elected government and the presence of international security forces in the country. According to a poll taken in late December 2006, just 10 percent of Afghans hold a favorable opinion of Muslim extremists, almost unchanged from 2004 and 2005. The same poll showed that 88 percent of Afghans prefer Karzai's government to the Taliban, with just 3 percent—mostly along the border with Pakistan—preferring the latter. As for foreign soldiers, three in four Afghans say they are grateful for the NATO troops in their country, and 88 percent say that the U.S.-led invasion to overthrow the Taliban was a good thing. Sixty percent of those polled said they wanted U.S. troops to stay in Afghanistan until security is restored.[41]

To ensure that the opportunity to save Afghanistan is not squandered, the first priority must be to provide financial and security assistance commensurate with the stakes, which America has so far failed to do. Indeed, despite Afghanistan's obvious importance, in the first two years following the fall of the Taliban it received the smallest amount of international financial and military assistance per capita of any recent U.S.-led postconflict rebuilding mission.[42] In 2002, the United States committed around $500 million in reconstruction aid to Afghanistan, compared to $18 billion for Iraq in 2003. And even when all international financial aid is taken into account, the average Afghan received about $50 in foreign aid during the first two years after the Taliban's ouster, one-tenth the amount received by Bosnians and one-twelfth the amount received by Kosovars over a comparable period.[43] President Bush's February 2007 request to Congress to provide $11.8 billion in support to Afghanistan over the next two years was a step in the right direction, but it must be funded by Congress, sustained, and matched by similar allied commitments if it is to succeed.

U.S. and allied military deployments to Afghanistan have also been insufficient. If NATO were to send as many troops per capita to Afghanistan as it did to Bosnia in 1995, it would have over 400,000 troops in the country; instead it has 36,000.[44] Such a massive deployment is obviously neither realistic nor necessary, but it does help to put calls by NATO commanders for a modest force increase into perspective. Especially if the United States withdraws more than 100,000 troops from Iraq, coming up with fewer than 10,000 more for Afghanistan should not be difficult and would help send a message to the Taliban and Afghan people in general that NATO is not going to withdraw.

Even more important than deploying additional international forces is the need to strengthen the Afghan National Army (ANA). Especially along the border with Pakistan, the authority of the Afghan government is being challenged by the Taliban, private security firms, and organized crime networks.[45] And the support of the Afghan people is up for grabs, based on who they think will win and in part on who can offer them better conditions. A larger and more robust NATO deployment could help with the first concern, while better pay and equipment for the ANA could help with the second. While the Taliban has the advantage of access to weapons and new recruits from safe havens in Pakistan, it is inexcusable for the international community to allow the ANA to lose to this competition. At present, Afghan soldiers earn less than $100 a month, whereas the Taliban pays its soldiers up to $300 a month. (By contrast, it costs NATO $4,000 a month to pay and maintain each of its soldiers.)[46]

Doubling the pay for all 32,000 members of the Afghan army would thus cost NATO around $3.2 million a month—roughly the cost of three of the Tomahawk cruise missiles used during the operation to overthrow the Taliban. Even tripling Afghan soldiers' pay would only amount to around $58 million per year, still a fraction of the alliance's $1.5 billion annual budget for Afghan operations or of the more than $14 billion the United States gave to Afghanistan between 2002 and 2007. Bolstering the ANA in this fashion would strengthen the Afghan army's capability, undercut Taliban recruitment, reduce the need for additional NATO forces, and potentially reduce Taliban motivation by forcing them to fight Afghan rather than NATO soldiers.[47]

Most important, America must vigorously address the issue of Pakistani support for the Taliban. In many ways Pakistan is itself the heart of the problem: it is the home of Taliban headquarters; the place where al Qaeda is reportedly reconstituting itself; the suspected hideout for Osama bin Laden, Ayman al-Zawahiri, and the former Taliban leader Mullah Omar; and the place to which aspiring Muslim terrorists from Europe travel for training or guidance.

Though in some ways Pakistan is an ally in the war on terror, in practice President Pervez Musharraf is pursuing a policy of "selective counterterrorism," in the words of former CIA official Bruce Riedel—operating against some groups but leaving others alone, and taking periodic action to appease the United States while at the same time protecting terrorist groups.[48] The former NATO Supreme Allied Commander James Jones notes that "evidence of Pakistan's complicity has been presented to . . . Musharraf by both U.S. and NATO commanders" but "the Musharraf government has been unhelpful in addressing the problems of porous borders." He adds, "Afghanistan is losing its struggle for stability and security in part because Pakistan cannot decide whether it wants to fight terrorism or encourage it as state policy."[49]

U.S. leverage over Pakistan is limited—Washington has long rightly feared that if Musharraf were ever ousted from power any regime that would replace him could be worse—but that does not mean America has no leverage. Indeed, since 9/11 the United States has given Pakistan over $10 billion in economic and military aid ($750 million in 2006), and threats to limit that aid were made more credible by the November 2006 election of a Democratic Congress that has expressed impatience with Pakistan's less than full cooperation.[50] When Vice President Cheney visited Islamabad in March 2007, reportedly to pressure Pakistan to do more to counter the Taliban's resurgence, a top Taliban official was arrested within hours of his visit. A senior Pakistani intelligence official called the arrest of Obaidullah Akhund, the former Taliban defense minister, a case of "pure coincidence and . . . good luck"—just the sort of coincidence and luck that American pressure on Islamabad has managed to produce in the past, and must in the future.[51] Pakistan can do better, and the United States must use all the tools at its disposal to ensure that it does.

But coercing Pakistan is not enough; the United States must also demonstrate to the Pakistanis the positive side of what cooperation can bring. By leveraging its economic and military aid along with its good relationship with India and diplomatic influence in the region, America needs to convince Pakistan that its relations with Washington are more important than its relations with the Taliban. The traditional Pakistani notion that it needed a strong Afghan client to provide "strategic depth" in a potential war against India is outmoded in a world where Pakistan boasts an overt nuclear deterrent and a confident and democratic India is ready to pursue détente and cooperation with its neighbors. Washington should facilitate this process by promoting regional diplomatic, economic, and energy ties—perhaps through a new four-power grouping of the United States, Afghanistan, Pakistan, and India. And it should use the current period of relative calm between India and Pakistan to promote a solution to the Kashmir problem, which would also be an enormous contribution in the fight against terrorism. A deal in which the current "line of control" in Kashmir becomes the permanent border between India and Pakistan and the Muslim areas of Kashmir constitute a special zone within India could form the basis for peace between the two nuclear neighbors. Such a step toward peace would enable Musharraf finally to shut down the many Pakistani extremist groups for whom Kashmir is their raison d'être and further undermine the perceived Pakistani need for a Taliban client in Afghanistan.

Finally, the United States must press Musharraf to restore civilian rule, as he has promised many times. Ironically, whereas the Bush administration has pushed strongly for elections in places where those elections were likely to and did produce Islamist majorities, it has been reluctant to do so in Pakistan, where fundamentalists have not fared well when put to the electoral test.

WINNING TURKEY BACK

The right war in the greater Middle East must not deal only with countries that have been long-standing problems and that we want as allies, but also with long-standing allies that we do not want to become problems. In this regard, no relationship is more important—or more at risk—than the one with the Republic of Turkey. For more than five decades, Turkey has been a stalwart NATO ally in the Cold War and a strategic partner of the United States. Today, however, Turkey is an increasingly resentful partner whose population increasingly doubts the value of a close link with the United States. Without the right policies from Washington, future U.S. leaders will be asking "Who lost Turkey?" and suffering the consequences of that outcome for years.

Perhaps even more than anywhere else in Europe or the Middle East, public opinion polls in Turkey tell a deeply de pressing story. In a poll conducted in 2000, 52 percent of Turkish respondents said they had a "favorable opinion" of the United States, a reflection of the countries' long-standing strategic partnership. By 2006, that number had fallen to just 12 percent, the lowest level among the twenty-three countries polled in the Pew Global Attitudes Survey.[52] In other polls, 91 percent of Turks said they disagreed with the foreign policies of the United States, 82 percent considered U.S. policies in the Middle East a "threat to peace and security," and twice as many respondents felt as warmly toward Iran as toward the United States.[53] When asked in 2006 who was Turkey's "best friend," 24 percent said "nobody," a reflection of many Turks' long-standing feeling that their country is misunderstood. But in contrast to past years, when the United States was at least a close second to "nobody," now the European Union was in second place at 19 percent, and the United States had fallen to 13 percent— barely ahead of Pakistan and "the Islamic world."[54] These negative attitudes toward the United States in particular and the West in general have been reflected in Turkish popular culture, with the huge success of books like Burak Turna's *Metal Storm* (a novel based on the premise of a U.S. invasion of Turkey) and blockbuster movies like *Valley of the Wolves* (about American brutality in Iraq).

There are many factors behind Turkey's strained relations with the United States, but the most important is Turkish resentment of U.S. policy in Iraq. The Iraq war has created a civil war on Turkey's southeastern border, threatened the security of Iraq's estimated one million Turkmen citizens, and contributed to the rise of Kurdish violence in Turkey after a period of relative calm. Many Turks resent Washington's refusal to heed their warnings about the consequences of going to war in Iraq, and the Turkish parliament's refusal to allow the U.S. Army's Fourth Infantry Division to pass through its territory during the invasion in 2003 is a clear example of the real costs of American unpopularity among democratic allies.

The potential threat from Turkey's estrangement from the United States is of a different character from the other countries discussed here, but the U.S. stake in Turkey's future is very high. Turkey is the most advanced democracy in the Islamic world, the home to more than 70 million Muslims, and it has borders with Armenia, Azerbaijan, Bulgaria, Georgia, Greece, Iran, Iraq, and Syria. It is the corridor through which the vast energy reserves of the Caspian Sea and Central Asia will pass to the West—the only alternative being Iran. A stable, Western-oriented, liberal Turkey on a clear path toward membership in the European Union would serve as a growing market for Western goods, a contributor to the labor forces Europe will desperately need, a democratic example for the rest of the Muslim world, a stabilizing influence on Iraq, a partner in Afghanistan, and a critical ally in the war on terrorism—not a bad list of attributes. A resentful, nationalistic, unstable, and protectionist Turkey, on the other hand, would be the opposite in every case. If its domestic politics go in this direction, Turkey not only could cease being a close friend but could become an adversary of the West or a source of terrorism.

To win Turkey back, the United States must deal with the Kurdish issue, which threatens Turkey's stability more than any other. Turkey's greatest fear is that an independent Kurdish state in northern Iraq would serve as a supplier and staging ground for Kurdish separatists in southeastern Turkey, where Kurds constitute the vast majority of the population. The United States must vigorously pursue a public antiterrorist campaign against Kurdish separatist parties in Turkey and use its considerable leverage with Iraq's Kurds to establish clear "redlines": no formal Kurdish independence, no support for irredentism, and respect for minority rights, including for the significant Turkmen community in northern Iraq. The United States should let Iraq's Kurds know that if these redlines are crossed, it would not be in a position to prevent Turkey from intervening militarily, which would be catastrophic for the entire Middle East, including the Kurds. The U.S. diplomatic objective should be to encourage the development of a stable Kurdish entity in

northern Iraq that would look to Turkey as a strategic partner and economic lifeline in a dangerous region, not as a
hostile neighbor.

The United States must also work to repair strained relations with Turkey in other areas. It can make more of an
effort to lessen the diplomatic and economic isolation of
the Turkish Cypriots, who in 2004 courageously—and
with Ankara's backing—supported a political settlement on
the long-divided island that the Greek side rejected. The U.S.
president should stand with Turkey in opposing efforts to
punish modern Turkey for an Ottoman "genocide" against Ar-
menians during World War I while encouraging Turkey hon-
estly to confront its past and to allow more freedom of
expression about these events. And the United States should
continue to encourage European Union leaders to keep the
door open to Turkey's eventual full membership. Everybody,
including the Turks, realizes that the path will be difficult and
that accession will not happen anytime soon. But those European leaders who had the strategic vision to promote Turkey's
candidacy in the first place need to continue to make the case
that a democratic, prosperous, and strong Turkey within the
EU is in Europe's self-interest. And that a resentful Turkey,
not rewarded for making progress on democracy, human
rights, and diplomatic issues, is not in their interest. It may
take a decade or more of efforts to make the strategic case for
Turkey's membership, expand EU-Turkey economic and security relations, and patiently explain to skeptical publics why
these developments are important. In a dangerous and unstable Middle East, we need to work not only to make stable
friends out of unstable adversaries but also to hold on to the
stable friends we already have.

★ ★ ★

The agenda outlined here is vast, yet far from complete. The right war in the Middle East will require new efforts to entice the Syrian regime to break its alliance with Iran, along with pressure on that regime to end its support for terrorism lest its economic and political isolation continue. It will require greater efforts to back the elected government in Lebanon, to compete better with Hezbollah for domestic support. It will require stronger economic and political support for Jordan, whose young King Abdullah could become the sort of enlightened Arab leader capable of promoting regional peace and providing hope to his people. It will require maintenance of close U.S. ties with the governments of Egypt and Saudi Arabia, as well as incentives for those countries to create more political space for opposition movements as they transition to likely new rulers in the coming years. The key to all these efforts is to move away from the misguided approach of the past few years, which assumed that the demonstration of American power and division of the world into simplistic categories of friends and enemies would strike a blow at the causes of terrorism—when in fact it did the opposite. The agenda outlined here is a difficult one, fraught with risk. But the stakes are enormous. Changing course now could not only help us out of the current morass, but in time lead to something much greater: victory in the war on terror.

5 ★ WHAT VICTORY WILL
LOOK LIKE

In the fall of 1987, two years before the dramatic events that would lead to the destruction of the Berlin Wall and the collapse of the Soviet Union, the Cold War historian John Lewis Gaddis wrote an essay in *The Atlantic Monthly* called "How the Cold War Might End." The Cold War, Gaddis observed, had become "a way of life." It had "been around for so long that it is a thoroughly familiar, if unwelcome, presence. . . . We have become so accustomed to this phenomenon—by now the dominant event in the lives of more than one generation of statesmen—that it simply does not occur to us to think about how it might end or, more to the point, how we would like it to end." Inspired by the then recent Intermediate Nuclear Forces Treaty, under which the United States and the Soviet Union agreed to abolish an entire category of nuclear weapons, Gaddis began to wonder whether something more fundamental was going on. He even imagined "the possibility that the Cold War itself—the occasion for deploying such vast quantities of nuclear armaments in the first place—might one day end," with the two superpowers negotiating peace, getting rid of their nuclear weapons, and working together cooperatively in a new international system."[1]

Gaddis's provocative essay, coming from someone who had written a number of books about the Cold War's evolution and who had every reason to believe that his subject would continue to give him professional fodder for years, was imaginative and courageous. Yet even in his own later reckoning, Gaddis's attempt to envisage the end of the Cold War merited no better than a C+. He deserved great credit for even asking the question, but he did not realize that the Cold War was already entering its final phase, that it would end with the complete and peaceful victory of one side, or that the Soviet Union might not only lose, but fall apart.[2]

Gaddis's exercise is a good warning to anyone reckless enough to venture thoughts—let alone predictions—about future developments in world politics. In the affairs of nations and individuals, too many variables are involved for even the sharpest observers to see the future with any confidence. This book is replete with examples of smart and well-informed people whose expectations, even about the near future, have already proven wildly off the mark.

Yet for all the perils involved in trying to look ahead, there is much to be gained in the effort. Indeed, any argument about policy options is at least implicitly based on predictive judgments about where those different options might lead. That is the very essence of strategy: to define an objective and then decide on the ways and means that are most likely to lead toward that goal and at what cost. Only by imagining different possible outcomes, and the different ways of achieving those outcomes, can we possibly assess the choices before us on issues so vital to our future.

The exercise must be done with particular humility on something as wide-ranging and amorphous as the war on terror. If we accept that this war is even partly analogous to the Cold War, and that the Cold War started around 1947, then we are just now entering 1953 on the Cold War calendar. Anyone then who would have even come close to imagining its later course—the ups and downs of détente, the Cuban Missile Crisis, or the Vietnam War, let alone the collapse of communism, the avoidance of nuclear war, and the peaceful disintegration of the Soviet Union—would have had to be either a visionary or exceedingly lucky. As predictions go, Kennan's observation that the Soviet Union would eventually "mellow" was about as good as it gets, but even this prescient diplomat would doubtless have admitted he had no idea how long that might take or what the process might actually look like.

What, then, can we say about the future of the war on terror? Will it ever end? How long will it take? What might victory (or defeat) look like? Would we recognize victory if it came, and would we see it coming?

IMAGINING THE FUTURE

One of the few predictions that can be made with even a modicum of confidence about the future of the war on terror is that it will, in fact, end. The main reason for this is that all wars eventually do end. Such an observation might appear flip, but there is a serious point behind it: the factors that underpin the structure of the international system— economic, technological, social, military, environmental, and ideological—are so numerous and so fluid that no political system or conflict can last forever. Thus, some wars end quickly (the Anglo-Zanzibar War of 1896 famously lasted for just forty-five minutes), and others endure (the Hundred Years' War, despite its name, lasted for 116 years). Some wars end relatively well (World War II laid the foundation for significant peace and prosperity), whereas others produce further catastrophe (World War I). But they all end, one way or another, and it behooves those living through them to imagine how and why their conclusions might be hastened and improved.

The Cold War is an excellent example of a war that ended at a time and in a way that almost all those who were living through it failed to foresee. For the first few years of the Cold War, its possible termination was not too far from the minds of those who were waging it. One possible scenario was a quick Western victory—preventive war against the prenuclear Soviet Union that would lead to the collapse of communism and the installation of a more congenial regime. Another scenario—scarier from the Western perspective but all too realistic—was Soviet victory. Indeed, those who were pushing most strongly to win the Cold War quickly did so because they feared losing it, as communism spread around the globe. By the early to mid-1950s, a third, even more frightening, way in which the Cold War might end was very much on the minds of Americans: with a nuclear war that would obliterate both sides.

By the mid-1960s, however, almost everyone, leaders and the public alike, started to lose sight of the possible end of the Cold War. Grudgingly, they began to focus instead on what became known as peaceful coexistence. The policy of détente, initiated in the 1960s and pursued throughout the

1970s, is sometimes retrospectively portrayed merely as a different way of bringing the Cold War to an end, but détente in reality was more a sign of resignation to the Cold War's expected endurance than an alternative way of concluding it. The primary objective of its proponents was to make the Cold War less dangerous, not to bring it to a seemingly improbable end. Ultimately, détente served to soften the image of the West in Soviet eyes, to civilize Soviet leaders through diplomatic interaction, and to lead Moscow into a dialogue about human rights that would end up undermining its legitimacy, all of which did contribute to the end of the Cold War. But this was not the main goal of the strategy.

Détente's critics, however, were also caught by surprise by the end of the Cold War. Ronald Reagan, it is true, denounced accommodation in the 1970s and 1980s and began to talk about defeating communism once and for all. But even Reagan's vision for burying communism was only a "plan and hope for the long-term," as he told the British Parliament in 1982.[3] Reagan admitted that when he declared, "Mr. Gorbachev, tear down this wall!" during a speech in Berlin in June 1987, he "never dreamed that in less than three years the wall would come down."[4] Reagan and his supporters, moreover, saw the Soviet Union of the late 1970s and early 1980s not as a failing empire in its final stages but as a powerful, threatening superpower whose expansion had to be checked. By the end of the 1980s, when the signs of the Soviet Union's internal rot and external softening were finally starting to become apparent, it was those who later claimed to have foreseen the end of the Cold War who steadfastly refused to accept that it was happening before their eyes. Even as the Soviet leader Mikhail Gorbachev began to undertake the reforms that would lead to the end of the confrontation with the United States, Americans and others had become so used to the Cold War as a "way of life," as Gaddis put it, that they had trouble recognizing what was happening. Hard-liners like Reagan defense official Richard Perle were still warning that Gorbachev had "imperial ambitions and an abiding attachment to military power" while "realists" like Brent Scowcroft, President George H. W. Bush's national security adviser, were "suspicious of [Gorbachev's] motives and skeptical about his prospects."[5] The CIA, whose job it was to identify important geopolitical trends, was still predicting as late as April 1989 that "for the foreseeable future, the USSR will remain the West's principal adversary," a view that was shared by the American public at large.[6] When asked in November 1989—the very month the Berlin Wall fell—whether they thought the Cold War had ended or not, only 18 percent said it was over, and 73 percent said it was not.[7] Ironically, it was only when the vast majority of Americans had finally given up on ever seeing the end of the Cold War that it actually came to an end.

Can we, today, do any better in anticipating how and when the war on terror might end? It is probably fair to assume that, like the Cold War, the war on terror will go on for a considerable amount of time. But assuming that it will not go on forever, what will the end of that war look like when it finally comes?

AFTER THE WAR ON TERROR

Just as it was possible to imagine the Soviet Union winning the Cold War, one theoretical possibility to be considered today would be the victory of al Qaeda. We in the West may not have an agreed theory of victory or path to get there, but Osama bin Laden and his cohorts certainly do. Bin Laden's goal, as he, his deputy Ayman al-Zawahiri, and others have often articulated, is to drive the United States out of Arab lands, topple the region's current rulers, and establish Islamic authority under a new caliphate. The path to this goal, they have made clear, is to "provoke and bait" the United States into "bleeding wars" on Muslim lands. Since Americans, they argue, do not have the stomach for a long and bloody fight, they will eventually give up and leave the region to its fate. Once the secular and autocratic regimes responsible for the Muslim world's humiliation have been removed, it will be possible to return Arab territory to the idealized state of Arabia at the time of Muhammad. The caliphate will be established from Morocco to Central Asia, Shari'a rule will prevail, Israel will be destroyed, oil prices will skyrocket, and the United States will recoil in humiliation and possibly even collapse —just as the Soviet Union did after the mujahideen defeated it in Afghanistan.[8]

Bin Laden's version of the end of the war on terror is a fantasy. It is based on an exaggeration of his own role in bringing down the Soviet Union, a failure to appreciate the long-term strength and adaptability of American society, and an underestimation of Muslim resistance to his extremist views. But if bin Laden's scenarios are misguided, they are also worth understanding and keeping in mind. For if we fail to appreciate his vision of how the war on terror could end, we may end up playing into his hands. We may inadvertently prolong the war by being drawn into the very battles that bin Laden believes will lead to our ruin and inspire Muslim support. These are

the errors that have led to America's unenviable position today in Iraq.

In the long run we remain far more likely to win this war
than al Qaeda, not only because liberty is ultimately more
appealing than a narrow and extremist interpretation of Islam, but because we will learn from our mistakes, while al
Qaeda's increasingly desperate efforts will alienate even its
potential supporters. But what will our victory look like? To
answer, we must first understand what victory will *not* look
like. Victory in the war on terror will not mean the "end of
terrorism," the "end of tyranny," or the "end of evil," utopian
goals that have all been articulated at one time or another.
Terrorism, after all (to say nothing of tyranny and evil), has
been around for a long time and will never go away entirely.
From the Sicarii and the Zealots in the first century to the
Assassins in the medieval period, the anarchists of the nine-
teenth century, and the Tamil Tigers, Red Brigades, Palestine Liberation Organization, Irish Republican Army, and
others in more recent times, terrorism has been a tactic
used by the weak in an effort to produce political change.[9]
Like violent crime, deadly disease, and other scourges, it
can be reduced and it can be contained, but it is unlikely
ever to be totally eliminated.

This is a critical point, because the goal of ending the risk
of terrorism entirely is not only unrealistic but also counterproductive, as would be the pursuit of other utopian goals.
We could, for example, vastly reduce, if not eliminate, mur-
der from the streets of Washington, D.C., by deploying several hundred thousand police officers there and authorizing
preventive detentions. We could eliminate traffic deaths in
the United States by reducing the national speed limit to ten

miles per hour. Or we could stop illegal immigration from Mexico by building a vast wall along the border and mandating the death penalty for undocumented workers. No sensible person would propose any of these measures, however, because the consequences of the "solutions" would be less acceptable than the risks themselves. The risk of terrorism in the United States could perhaps be similarly reduced if we reallocated billions of dollars per year in domestic spending to homeland security measures, significantly curtailed civil liberties to ensure that no potential terrorists were on the streets, and invaded and occupied countries that might one day support or sponsor terrorism. Pursuing that goal in this way, however, would have costs that would vastly outweigh the benefits of reaching the goal, even if reaching it were possible. In their book *An End to Evil*, former Bush speechwriter David Frum and defense adviser Richard Perle insist there is "no middle ground" and that "Americans are not fighting this evil to minimize it or to manage it." The choice, they say, comes down to "victory or holocaust."[10] Thinking in these terms, however, is likely to lead the United States into a series of wars, abuses, and overreactions more likely to perpetuate the war on terror than to bring it to a successful end. We would do better to purge from our minds the paradigm of total victory, in which the adversary capitulates, signs a truce, or disappears. The war on terror is not a traditional war and it will not have a traditional ending.

But that does not mean the war on terror will not end or that we cannot realistically win it. On the contrary, if we learn to fight the right war we will win, and the war on terror will end with the collapse of the violent ideology that caused it. The war will end, in other words, when the bin Laden

comes to be seen by its potential adherents as a fail-
when they turn against it and adopt other means and
go s. The romantics and idealists who saw bin Ladenism as
a path to salvation for themselves and their religion will
come to recognize that it cannot deliver, and they will turn
to different strategies and alternative dreams. In this sense,
the death of extremist Islamism will be analogous to that of
communism, which itself once seemed vibrant and attractive to millions around the world, but which over time came
to be seen as an illegitimate failure. Just as Lenin and
Stalin's successors in the Kremlin in the mid-1980s finally
came to the realization that they would never accomplish
their goals if they did not radically change course, it is not
too fanciful to imagine the successors of bin Laden and al-
Zawahiri a generation from today reflecting on that movement's accomplishments—or rather, its failures—and
coming to the same conclusion. The ideology will not have
been destroyed by American military power, but its adherents may well decide that the path they have chosen can
never lead them where they want to go. And to paraphrase
Reagan, bin Laden's violent ideology will end up on the ash
heap of history, alongside Lenin's. Like communism today,
extremist Islamism in the future will have a few adherents
here and there. But as an organized ideology capable of taking over states or inspiring large numbers of people, it will
have been effectively dismantled, discredited, and discarded.

The world after the end of the war on terror will have several other characteristics. After the war on terror, the global
al Qaeda organization will no longer exist. Smaller, uncoor-
dinated, "copycat" organizations, still capable of carrying

out attacks, might, but the international conglomerate that was able to carry out such destruction on September 11, 2001, will not. Its leaders will have been killed or captured, its sanctuaries denied or destroyed, its financial sources tracked and blocked, and its communications interrupted or driven underground. Terrorism will not be over, but its central sponsor and most dangerous executor will be.

After the war on terror, American society will be better able to deny the remaining terrorists the ability to reach their primary goal: terror. The risk of attack will still exist, but if an attack takes place it will not provoke a dramatic foreign policy revolution or the restriction of the sorts of civil liberties that make America what it is and ought to be. As in other societies that have faced terrorism (the United Kingdom, Israel, India, and others), life will go on and people will go about their daily business without inordinate fear. The terrorists will see that the result of any attack was not the overreaction they sought to provoke but rather the stoic denial of their ability to provoke a counterproductive response. Put in the hands of the U.S. legal system and locked away for years after due legal process, they will be seen as the heartless criminals they are rather than as the valiant soldiers they seek to be. Over time, the risk of attack will become even lower or attacks will practically stop altogether, because they will not serve their intended purpose. The change in the nation's psychology will be like the change that has taken place in New York City since 1990, when the rate of violent crime was some 75 percent greater than it is today. New Yorkers still run some risk of being attacked when they go out at night, but it has ceased to be a matter of everyday concern requiring a change of lifestyle.

After the war on terror, the nation's priorities will come back into balance. Preventing terrorism will remain an important goal, but it will no longer have to be the predominant paradigm for U.S. foreign policy. Instead, it will take its place as just one of several concerns for American citizens, alongside health care, the environment, education, and the economy. Budgets, speeches, elections, and policies will no longer revolve around the war on terror to the exclusion of other critical issues on which the nation's welfare depends.

We are a long way from this world. The political and economic stagnation in the Middle East, the war in Iraq, the Arab-Israel struggle, and other conflicts from Kashmir to Chechnya continue to produce the frustration and humiliation that cause terrorism, and it only takes a small number of extremists to pose a serious threat. But though the end of the war on terror will not come tomorrow, the paths that lead to it can already be seen. The disruption of the al Qaeda organization, for example, is well under way, and with determination and the right policies, that organization can be defeated. Bin Laden and al-Zawahiri are now living like fugitives in caves rather than like presidents or military commanders in villas in Afghanistan. Other top leaders have been killed or captured, and the organization's abilities to communicate globally and finance major operations have been significantly reduced. Al Qaeda is trying to reconstitute itself along the Afghanistan-Pakistan border, but with so much of the world—China, Russia, Europe, Saudi Arabia, Iran—sharing an interest in suppressing the group, it will have great difficulty ever becoming again the multinational global terrorist enterprise that was able to take America by surprise on 9/11.

We can also see signs of Muslim reaction against al Qaeda's use of wanton violence as a political tool—the sort of development that will be critical in the long-term effort to discredit jihadism. After al Qaeda's suicide attacks at two hotels in Jordan in November 2005—which killed some sixty civilians, including thirty-eight at a wedding party— Jordanians poured out into the streets to protest in record numbers. Subsequent public opinion polls showed that the portion of Jordanian respondents who believed that violence against civilian targets to defend Islam is *never* justified jumped from 11 to 43 percent, and those expressing a lot of confidence in Osama bin Laden to "do the right thing" plunged from 25 percent to less than 1 percent.[11] Similar Muslim reactions following al Qaeda attacks have taken place in Indonesia, Egypt, Pakistan, and Saudi Arabia.[12] In Iraq's Anbar province there are also signs that locals are getting fed up with Islamic terrorists and turning against them. In Spring 2007, 25 of 31 Sunni tribes from that region formed a coalition called Anbar Awakening, and began challenging al Qaeda militants operating there. Tribes that once welcomed al Qaeda support in the insurgency against U.S. forces are now fighting al Qaeda with thousands of fighters and significant local support.[13]

All this is why Marc Sageman, a former CIA psychiatrist who has studied Islamist terrorist movements, argues that support for jihadists will eventually erode just as it did for previous terrorist movements, like the anarchists of nineteenth-century Europe. In the long term, Sageman argues, "the militants will keep pushing the envelope and committing more atrocities to the point that the dream will no longer be attractive to young people."[14] Terrorism analyst Peter

Bergen also believes that violence that kills other Muslims will ultimately prove to be al Qaeda's Achilles' heel. Killing Muslims, he argues, is "doubly problematic for Al Qaeda, as the Koran forbids killing both civilians *and* fellow Muslims."[15] After the 9/11 attacks, wide segments of the Arab public and the media expressed sympathy with the victims, and prominent clerics (including Yusuf al-Qaradawi, a prominent firebrand Islamist with a wide following on satellite television) issued fatwas condemning the attacks as contrary to Islam and calling for the apprehension and punishment of the perpetrators.[16] That is what will have to happen if Islamist terrorism is to be discredited and discarded, and it is what will happen when the terrorists overreach and fail.

As a broader political ideology, fundamentalist Islam also has poor long-term prospects. Far from representing a political system likely to attract increasing numbers of adherents, fundamentalism has failed everywhere it has been tried. In Afghanistan under the Taliban, in Iran under the mullahs, in Sudan under the National Islamic Front, different strains of Islamist rule have produced economic failure and public discontent. Indeed, the Taliban and Iranian clerics are probably responsible for creating two of the most pro-American populations in the greater Middle East. Opinion polls also show that there is even less support for the kind of fundamentalist Islamic government proposed by bin Laden. "Many people would like bin Laden . . . to hurt America," says the political scientist and pollster Shibley Telhami, "but they do not want bin Laden to rule their children." Asked in Telhami's survey what, if any, aspect of al Qaeda they sympathized with, 33 percent of Muslims said none, 33 percent

said confronting the United States, 14 percent said support
for Muslim causes like the Palestinian issue, 11 percent
said al Qaeda's methods of operation, and only 7 percent
said they sympathized with its efforts to create an Islamic
state.[17] Fundamentalist Islam has not yet run its course and
cannot be expected to do so in less than a generation. Communism, after all, was a serious competitor to the capitalist
West for more than a century and survived in the Soviet
Union for more than seventy years. Communism was re-
silient enough to last for several decades even after its failings became clear to those who once embraced it, before
finally being discarded. In the long run, fundamentalist Islam is likely to suffer a similar fate.[18]

Finally, there are good reasons to believe that the forces
of globalization and communication that have been unleashed by changing technology will eventually produce
change in the Middle East as well. This will especially be
true if we succeed in promoting the sort of economic development in the region advocated in this book, which would
produce the middle classes who in other parts of the world
have often been the drivers of democratization. But even in
the absence of rapid economic change it is clear that increasingly open media created by the Internet and other
communications technologies can prove to be powerful
agents of change. Though only around 10 percent of households in the Arab world have access to the Internet, that
percentage is growing dramatically, having risen five-fold
since 2000. Even in Saudi Arabia, one of the most closed
and conservative societies in the world, there are over two
thousand bloggers, half of whom are women, whose blogs
are reportedly "filled with feminist poetry, steamy romantic

episodes and rants against their restricted lives and patriarchal society," according to a report in the *Washington Post*.[19] The spread of satellite television can also be a powerful force for change. Cable news stations like the independent Qatar-based Al Jazeera, the Dubai-based Al Arabiya—and even the U.S.-sponsored Al Hurra—reach tens of millions of households throughout the Arab world, often with information or perspectives the repressive governments in the region would rather not be heard. According to the Arab media expert Marc Lynch, "The conventional wisdom that the Arab media simply parrot the official line of the day no longer holds true. Al Jazeera has infuriated virtually every Arab government at one point or another, and its programming allows for criticism, and even mockery. Commentators regularly dismiss the existing Arab regimes as useless, self-interested, weak, compromised, corrupt, and worse." Lynch points out that one Al Jazeera talk show addressed the issue "Have the existing Arab regimes become worse than colonialism?" The host, one of the guests, and 76 percent of callers said yes—"marking a degree of frustration and inwardly directed anger that presents an opening for progressive change."[20]

That sort of progressive change is unlikely to take place in the near future, and it is true that the region's autocrats seem ever more determined to prevent it. But is it impossible that the next generation of leaders in Saudi Arabia, Egypt, Syria, Pakistan, or Iran will be forced to accept some form of progressive change? Middle Eastern leaders' priority will remain what it has been, to keep a grip on power, but what if it becomes clear that the only way to hold on to power is to change? What if they conclude that in the absence of change their regime might fall to fundamentalists, or that their country would be surpassed by regional rivals like Iran? There does not seem to be a Mikhail Gorbachev on the horizon at present, but that was also true for the Soviet Union as late as 1984. Gorbachev's immediate predecessors, Yuri Andropov and Konstantin Chernenko, did not seem to be harbingers of radical change when they passed through the Kremlin, but that is exactly what they were. A new, dynamic, and determined leader of a major Arab country who opens up political space and uses economic reform to make his country more powerful and prosperous may strike a greater blow in the fight against terrorism than anything the United States can ever do.

WRONG WAR, RIGHT WAR

While it is clear that victory in the war on terror is possible, and even probable, it is equally clear that the current approach is not likely to succeed. The Bush administration's assumption after 9/11 was that the toppling of Saddam Hussein in Iraq would set off a regional chain reaction that would ultimately make the United States safer. A key supporter of terrorism would be eliminated, hostile regimes like Iran and Syria would be cowed, people throughout the region would aspire to live in free and flourishing democracies like the one Iraq was supposed to become, and the terrorists who attacked the United States would thereby be defeated.

The war on terror has not gone as planned because President Bush launched the wrong war. He argued and acted as if the problem was the terrorists' hatred for freedom, when in fact resentment, humiliation, and the unsolved diplomatic crises in the region were far more important. He sought to solve a major part of the problem with the overwhelming deployment of American military force, when in fact the demonstration of force only played into the terrorists' hands. He conflated a vast array of diverse threats into a single war on terror, thus making it impossible for the United States to prioritize among them or play one threat off another. He acted as if America's moral authority in the world was not open to challenge, when in fact efforts to preserve and demonstrate that moral authority could have been a key tool in isolating the terrorists. He hyped the terrorist threat as a means of winning political support for his efforts, when doing so only helped them achieve their goal of terrorizing and baiting America into counterproductive actions. He told potential allies that they had to be "with us" or "with the terrorists," failing to realize that that they might not automatically see the inherent purity of American motives, that they might have their own distinct and legitimate interests, or indeed that America might not always be right. And while he talked of a war that challenged the nation's very existence, he fought it on the cheap, as if he knew that Americans would not have been on board had they been told what the war would entail.

If we remain on the current course, we will create more terrorists than we kill or capture, and we will fuel the hatred that sustains them. We will unify our enemies, squander our resources, and undermine our most precious values. We will lose our allies, and we will lose our faith in ourselves. As we fail to accomplish our goals, pursuing the illusion that we can win by upping the ante—by attacking Syria or Iran, for example, or suddenly undercutting the regimes in Egypt or Saudi Arabia—may very well make things worse. On the current course, we will keep expanding the fight and keep getting surprised when stability and sympathy for the West does not result, and the terrorist threat does not go away and the struggle saps our strength.

An alternative course of action is possible—and necessary. By fighting the right war, we will show confidence in our own values and society, and the determination to preserve both. We will act decisively to reestablish our moral authority, which has been so badly damaged in recent years. We will strengthen our defenses against the terrorist threat, while also realizing that a "one percent" policy designed to prevent any conceivable attack does more damage than a policy of defiantly refusing to allow terrorists to change our way of life. We will expand our efforts to promote education and political and economic change in the Middle East, which in the long run will lead that region out of the despair and humiliation that fuel the terrorist threat. We will launch a major program to wean ourselves off imported oil from the region, freeing ourselves from the dependence that constrains our foreign policy and helping Muslim countries emerge from the curse that prevents their modernization and development. We will stop pretending that our disengagement from efforts to achieve peace between Israel and its neighbors has nothing to do with the problem of terrorism, and we will launch a diplomatic offensive designed to bring an end to this conflict that is so tragic for all sides. We will take seriously the views of our potential allies, we will recognize their legitimate interests, and we will seek to win their support and cooperation in confronting the common threat.

If we fight the right war, we must have confidence that in

the long run we will prevail. Ultimately, Islamism is not an ideology likely to win enduring support. Terrorism is not a strategy with which Muslims will forever want to be associated, and it will create a backlash within Muslim societies. With time and experience—and if we make the right choices—Muslims themselves will turn against the extremists in their midst. Somewhere in the Islamic world, at some point possibly sooner than we realize, new Lech Walesas, Václav Havels, and Andrei Sakharovs will emerge to reclaim their people's future from those who have hijacked it. They will seek to put their civilization on a path that will restore its greatest era—when the Islamic world was a multicultural zone of tolerance and of intellectual, artistic, and scientific achievement. The agents of change might come from above— like Mikhail Gorbachev, who used his position at the top of the Soviet hierarchy to transform the Soviet Union and end the Cold War. Or they might rise up from below—like the protesters in 1989 in Gdansk, Leipzig, and Budapest, who stood up against tyranny and reclaimed their future. If we are strong, smart, and patient, they will come. And they, not the West, will transform their world—and ours.

★ ★ ★ Notes

INTRODUCTION

1. Max Boot, "It's Not Over Yet," *Time*, September 9, 2006.

2. See White House, "Press Conference by the President," October 25, 2006, http://www.whitehouse.gov/news/releases/2006/10/20061025.html; and "Interview of the Vice President by Tim Russert, NBC News, Meet the Press," September 10, 2006, http://www.whitehouse.gov/news/releases/2006/09/20060910.html "Significant progress" quote is from Dick Cheney.

3. Newt Gingrich, "Bush and Lincoln," *Wall Street Journal*, September 7, 2006. Other commentators use the expression "World War IV," based on the notion that the Cold War was World War III. See Eliot A. Cohen, "World War IV: Let's Call This Conflict What It Is," *Wall Street Journal*, November 20, 2001; Norman Podhoretz, "How to Win World War IV," *Commentary*, February 1, 2002; Podhoretz, "World War IV: How It Started, What It Means, and Why We Have to Win," *Comentary*, September 1, 2002; and Podhoretz, "The War Against World War IV," *Commentary*, February 1, 2005.

4. Bush's first reference to a "war against terrorism" was in his televised address on the evening of September 11, 2001, when he said that America and its allies stood together to "win the war against terrorism." Nine days later, Bush declared to a joint session of Congress that the "war on terror" would "begin with al Qaeda, but . . . not end until every terrorist group of global reach has been

found, stopped and defeated." See White House, "Statement by the President in His Address to the Nation," September 11, 2001, http://www.whitehouse.gov/news/releases/2001/09/20010911 -16.html; and "Address to a Joint Session of Congress and the American People," September 20, 2001, http://www.white house.gov/news/releases/2001/09/20010920-8.html. For critics of the concept of a "war on terror," see Michael Howard, "What's in a Name? How to Fight Terrorism," *Foreign Affairs* (January–February 2002); and Zbigniew Brzezinski, *The Choice: Global Domination or Global Leadership* (New York: Basic Books, 2004), 27–28.

1: THE WRONG WAR

1. As former Reagan chief of staff Kenneth Duberstein put it, "For the past six years, every time the president gave a speech, people said it was the most important speech of his presidency. This is the most important speech." Quoted in Sheryl Gay Stolberg, "Bush Scrambling to Turn Around His Presidency," *International Herald Tribune*, January 8, 2007.
2. According to the Brookings Institution's Iraq Index there were 34,452 Iraqi civilian casualties in 2006. See Michael E. O'Hanlon and Jason H. Campbell, "Iraq Index: Tracking Variables of Reconstruction & Security in Post-Saddam Iraq," http://www.brookings.edu/iraqindex (accessed January 29, 2007).
3. James A. Baker III and Lee H. Hamilton, co-chairs, and Lawrence S. Eagleberger, Vernon E. Jordan Jr., Edwin Meese III, Sandra Day O'Connor, Leon E. Panetta, William J. Perry, Charles S. Robb, Alan K. Simpson, *The Iraq Study Group Report* (Washington, D.C.: United States Institute for Peace, 2006).
4. On the new direction of foreign policy in Bush's second term, see Philip H. Gordon, "The End of the Bush Revolution," *Foreign Affairs* (July–August 2006); Mike Allen and Romesh Ratnesar, "The End of Cowboy Diplomacy," *Time*, July 9, 2006; and Michael Abramowitz, "Conservative Anger Grows Over Bush's Foreign Policy," *Washington Post*, July 19, 2006.
5. White House, "President's Address to the Nation," January 10, 2007, http://www.whitehouse.gov/news/releases/2007/01/20070110-7 .html.

6. Gerard Baker, "Startling and Clear: Bush Defies Critics," Real Clear Politics Web site, January 11, 2007, http://www.realclearpolitics .com/articles/2007/01/startling_and_clear_bush_rejec.html.

7. George W. Bush, "Address to a Joint Session of Congress and the American People," September 20, 2001, http://www.whitehouse.gov/ news/releases/2001/09/20010920-8.html.

8. White House, "President Bush Discusses Global War on Terror," Wardman Park Marriott Hotel, Washington, D.C., September 29, 2006, http://www.whitehouse.gov/news/releases/2006/09/200609 29-3.html.

9. Pew Research Center for the People and the Press, "Views of a Changing World," June 2003, http://people-press.org/reports/ display.php3?ReportID=185, quoted in Scott Atran, "Mishandling Suicide Terrorism," *Washington Quarterly* (Summer 2004). Also see Mark Tessler, "Do Islamic Orientations Influence Attitudes Toward Democracy in the Arab World?: Evidence from Egypt, Jordan, Morocco, and Algeria," *International Journal of Comparative Sociology* 2 (Spring 2002): 229–49; and Mark Tessler and Dan Corstange, "How Should Americans Understand Arab and Muslim Political Attitudes?: Combating Stereotypes with Public Opinion Data from the Middle East," *Journal of Social Affairs* (Winter 2002).

10. Khalil Shikaki, "Palestinians Divided," *Foreign Affairs* (January– February 2002); Palestinian Center for Policy and Survey Research, "Public Opinion Poll No. 9," October 7–14, 2003, http:// www.pcpsr.org/survey/polls/2003/p9a.html.

11. F. Gregory Gause III, "Can Democracy Stop Terrorism?" *Foreign Affairs* (September–October 2005).

12. For the years 2000–3, see Gause, "Can Democracy Stop Terrorism?" In 2004, the U.S. government changed its methodology for tracking terrorist attacks and began to compile data on much more inclusive "incidents of terrorism" rather than the narrower "major terrorist attacks" counted in the State Department's *Patterns of Global Terrorism*. The data for 2004–5 thus reflect this wider category, but the general pattern is the same. See National Counterterrorism Center, "A Chronology of Significant International Terrorism for 2004," April 27, 2005; and Worldwide Incidents Tracking System, National Counterterrorism Center, http://wits.nctc.gov/Main.do, for the 2005 data (accessed

December 27, 2006). For data going back much further but show-
ing the same pattern, see William Eubank and Leonard Weinberg,
"Terrorism and Democracy: Perpetrators and Victims," *Terrorism
and Political Violence* 13/11 (Spring 2001): 155–64; and Quan Li,
"Does Democracy Promote or Reduce Transnational Terrorist
Incidents?" *Journal of Conflict Resolution* 49/2 (2005): 278–97.

13. Peter Bergen, "Briefing Notes: What Were the Causes of 9/11?"
Prospect, September 2006, 51.

14. Associated Press, "Text of Osama bin Laden's Statement," first
broadcast October 7, 2001.

15. Michael Powell, "Bin Laden Recruits with Graphic Video,"
Washington Post, September 27, 2001. On the role of perceived
injustice and humiliation in terrorism more generally, see Daniel
Benjamin and Steven Simon, *The Age of Sacred Terror* (New York:
Random House, 2002); Jessica Stern, *Terror in the Name of God*
(New York: HarperCollins, 2003); Olivier Roy, *Globalized Islam:
The Search for a New Ummah* (New York: Columbia University
Press, 2004); and Louise Richardson, *What Terrorists Want* (New
York: Random House, 2006).

16. Office of the Director of National Intelligence, "Declassified Key
Judgments of the National Intelligence Estimate: Trends in
Global Terrorism: Implications for the United States," April 2006,
http://www.dni.gov/press_releases/Declassified_NIE_Judgments.
pdf (accessed December 15, 2006).

17. Dame Eliza Manningham-Buller, director general of the Security
Service, "The International Terrorist Threat to the UK," speech at
Queen Mary's College, London, November 9, 2006, available at:
http://www.mi5.gov.uk.

18. Robert A. Pape, *Dying to Win: The Strategic Logic of Suicide
Terrorism* (New York: Random House, 2005); and Cato Institute,
"Suicide Terrorism and Democracy: What We've Learned Since
9/11," Policy Analysis no. 582, November 1, 2006.

19. George W. Bush, "Address to a Joint Session of Congress and the
American People," September 20, 2001, http://www.whitehouse
.gov/news/releases/2001/09/20010920-8.html.

20. White House, "President Bush Meets with Military Personnel at
Fort Campbell," Fort Campbell, Ky., March 18, 2004, http://
www.whitehouse.gov/news/releases/2004/03/20040318-3.html.

21. White House, "President Bush Delivers Graduation Speech at West Point," United States Military Academy, West Point, N.Y., June 1, 2002, http://www.whitehouse.gov/news/releases/2002/06/20020601-3.html.

22. White House, "President Bush Discusses Global War on Terror," Wardman Park Marriott Hotel, Washington, D.C., September 29, 2006, http://www.whitehouse.gov/news/releases/2006/09/20060929-3.html.

23. White House, "President Discusses War on Terror and Hurricane Preparation," Pentagon, September 22, 2005, http://www.whitehouse.gov/news/releases/2005/09/20050922.html.

24. White House, "Vice President's Remarks to Marines at Camp Lejeune," Camp Lejeune, N.C., October 3, 2005, http://www.whitehouse.gov/news/releases/2005/10/20051003-4.html.

25. See Edward Alden and Roula Khalaf, "Dealing with Gadaffi," *Financial Times,* London ed., October 28, 2003; Ray Takeyh, "The Rogue Who Came In from the Cold," *Foreign Affairs* (May–June, 2001), 62–72; and Martin Indyk, "The War Did Not Force Gaddaffi's Hand," *Financial Times,* March 9, 2004.

26. In his December 15, 2006, farewell speech after resigning as defense secretary, Rumsfeld stated: "It should be clear not only that weakness is provocative, but the perception of weakness on our part can be provocative as well." Quoted in Jim Rutenberg, "In Farewell, Rumsfeld Warns Weakness Is 'Provocative,'" *New York Times,* December 16, 2006. It was the same message Rumsfeld had been conveying since 2001, when he argued that "weakness is provocative . . . it kind of invites people to do things that they otherwise wouldn't think about doing." Quoted in Bill Gertz, "Rumsfeld Says U.S. Presence in Asia Is Vital," *Washington Times,* July 25, 2001.

27. According to an April 2006 official U.S. National Intelligence Estimate, the Iraq conflict has become "the *cause célèbre* for jihadists, breeding a deep resentment of U.S. involvement in the Muslim world and cultivating supporters for the global jihadist movement." See Office of the Director of National Intelligence, "Declassified Key Judgments of the National Intelligence Estimate: Trends in Global Terrorism: Implications for the United States," April 2006, http://www.dni.gov/press_releases/Declassified_NIE_

Key_Judgments.pdf (accessed December 15, 2006); as well as Daniel Benjamin and Steven Simon, "Of Course Iraq Made It Worse," *Washington Post,* September 29, 2006.

28. Quoted in Mark Danner, "Taking Stock of the Forever War," *The New York Times Magazine,* September 1, 2005.

29. Osama bin Laden's October 29, 2004, "The Towers of Lebanon" tape, quoted in Danner, "Taking Stock."

30. Thomas Ricks, *Fiasco: The American Military Adventure in Iraq* (New York: Penguin, 2006).

31. Lewis E. Lehrman and William Kristol, "Crush the Insurgents in Iraq," *Washington Post,* May 23, 2004.

32. U.S. Department of the Army, *Counterinsurgency,* Field Manual No. 3-24, Marine Corps Warfighting Publication No. 3-33.5, Washington, D.C., December 15, 2006, par. 1–45. Also see James Dobbins and Philip H. Gordon, "Gaining the Iraqis' Toleration," *Washington Post,* May 28, 2004.

33. For the State Department recommendation, see Colin L. Powell, "Memorandum re Draft Decision Memorandum for President on the Applicability of the Geneva Convention to the Conflict in Afghanistan," January 26, 2002, http://www.humanrightsfirst.org/us_law/etn/gonzales/memos_dir/memo_20020126_Powell_WH%20.pdf.

34. This was the view of Lord Johan Steyn, a member of Britain's highest court, who added, "As a lawyer brought up to admire the ideals of American democracy and justice, I would have to say that I regard this as a monstrous failure of justice." See Lord Johan Steyn, remarks to the British Institute of International and Comparative Law, Twenty-seventh F. A. Mann Lecture, November 25, 2003, available at: http://www.barhumanrights.org.uk/pdfs/FA_Mann_lecture1Dec03.pdf.

35. Assistant Attorney General Jay S. Bybee, "Memorandum for Alberto R. Gonzales, Counsel to the President, re Standards of Conduct for Interrogation Under 18 U.S.C. §§2340-2340A," August 1, 2002, http://fl1.findlaw.com/news.findlaw.com/nytimes/docs/doj/bybee80102mem.pdf. Repr. in Karen J. Greenberg and Joshua L. Dratel, *The Torture Papers: The Road to Abu Ghraib* (New York: Cambridge University Press, 2005), 172–217.

36. The Bybee memo (n. 35) as well as the discussion in Joseph Margulies, *Guantánamo and the Abuse of Presidential Power* (New York: Simon & Schuster, 2006), 90.

37. In *Rasul v. Bush,* a case that involved an Australian and two British citizens captured in Afghanistan, the Court rejected the Bush administration's argument that U.S. law had no jurisdiction in Guantánamo, ruling that even non-U.S. prisoners there should have access to the court system. In *Hamdi v. Rumsfeld,* a case that involved a U.S. citizen captured in Afghanistan, the Court ruled that the administration had the right to declare U.S. citizens "enemy combatants" but that such prisoners had to be able to appeal that designation before an impartial judge.

38. U.S. Supreme Court, *Hamdi et al. v. Rumsfeld et al.,* October Term, argued April 28, 2004, decided June 28, 2004.

39. The story was broken by the CBS newsmagazine *60 Minutes II,* which aired its report on April 28, 2004, and by Seymour Hersh, whose article "Torture at Abu Ghraib" was posted online April 30 and appeared in *The New Yorker* of May 10, 2004. Also see Seymour Hersh, *Chain of Command: The Road from 9/11 to Abu Ghraib* (New York: HarperCollins, 2004); and Major General Antonio M. Taguba, "The Taguba Report on Treatment of Abu Ghraib Prisoners in Iraq," Article 15–6, Investigation of the 800th Military Police Brigade, http://news.findlaw.com/hdocs/docs/iraq/tagubarpt.html.

40. "The Taguba Report" and Kate Zernike, "Detainees Depict Abuses by Guard in Prison in Iraq," *New York Times,* January 12, 2005.

41. "Homicide Unpunished," *Washington Post,* February 28, 2006.

42. Bush administration lawyers tried to argue that such an approach would be legal, since the Senate, when it ratified the UN Convention Against Torture in 1994, had linked the definition of mistreatment to the Eighth Amendment of the U.S. Constitution, which applies only to U.S. citizens. However, Abraham Sofaer, who had served as the legal adviser to the State Department when the Convention was signed, insisted that the obvious purpose of linking the definition to the Constitution was to give "cruel, inhuman and degrading treatment" the same meaning as "cruel and unusual punishment" in the Eighth Amendment, not to constrain the geographic reach of the Convention. See Abraham D. Sofaer

to Hon. Patrick J. Leahy, January 21, 2005, letter cited in Margulies, *Guantánamo*, 179. Also see David Luban, "Torture, American-Style," *Washington Post*, November 27, 2005. On Cheney's efforts to exempt the CIA, see David Espo and Liz Sidoti, "Cheney Appeals to GOP Senators for CIA Exemption to Torture Ban," Associated Press, November 4, 2005. The *Washington Post* noted that Bush's veto threat meant that he was "proposing to use the first veto of his presidency on a defense bill needed to fund military operations in Iraq and Afghanistan so that he can preserve the prerogative to subject detainees to cruel, inhuman and degrading treatment." See "End the Abuse," *Washington Post*, October 7, 2005.

43. White House, "President's Signing Statement, HR2863," CQ Federal Department and Agency Documents, December 30, 2005.

44. White House, "President Discusses Creation of Military Commissions to Try Suspected Terrorists," September 6, 2006, http://www.whitehouse.gov/news/releases/2006/09/2006090 6-3.html. ABC News reported that the practices included "water boarding," extreme sleep deprivation, and forced standing of up to forty hours, all of which have long been condemned as torture by the U.S. government. Brian Ross and Richard Esposito, "CIA's Harsh Interrogation Techniques Described," ABC News, November 18, 2005.

45. For Gonzales, Jackson Diehl, "Inhuman: Yes or No?" *Washington Post*, September 12, 2005. Also see "Minced Words; Torture," *The Economist*, December 10, 2005.

46. Olivier Roy, "We're Winning, Despite the 'War,'" *International Herald Tribune*, September 7, 2006.

47. For the Wolfowitz quote, DOD, News Briefing—Deputy Secretary Wolfowitz, Pentagon, September 13, 2001, http://www .defenselink.mil/transcripts/transcript.aspx?transcriptid=1622. On Woolsey's trip, Karen DeYoung and Rick Weiss, "U.S. Seems to Ease Rhetoric on Iraq; Officials Urge Wait and See on Anthrax," *Washington Post*, October 24, 2001. The article quotes Woolsey saying, "There are too many things, too many examples of stolen identities, of cleverly crafted documentation, of coordination across continents and between states . . . to stray very far

from the conclusion that a state, and a very well-run intelligence service, is involved here."

48. That thesis is expounded in Laurie Mylroie, *The War Against America: Saddam Hussein and the World Trade Center Attacks*, 2nd rev. ed. (New York: Regan Books, 2000); the book jacket includes glowing blurbs from Wolfowitz, Perle, and Woolsey. The lack of solid evidence for Mylroie's thesis is discussed in Peter Bergen, "Armchair Provocateur: Laurie Mylroie: The Neocons' Favorite Conspiracy Theorist," *Washington Monthly*, December 1, 2003.

49. Ken Adelman, "Cakewalk in Iraq," *Washington Post*, February 13, 2006.

50. Quoted in Nicholas Lemann, "After Iraq," *The New Yorker*, February 17, 2003, 72. Several years later, Feith was still arguing that the Iraq war was "an operation to prevent the next, as it were, 9/11." Jeffrey Goldberg, "A Little Learning: What Douglas Feith Knew and When He Knew It," *The New Yorker*, May 9, 2005.

51. In September 2006, 43 percent of those surveyed believed Saddam Hussein was "personally involved" with 9/11, and 46 percent said there was a "connection" between Iraq and the attacks. See "Poll: Iraq War Could Wound GOP at Polls," September 25, 2006, http://www.cnn.com/2006/POLITICS/09/06/iraq.poll/index.html for the first figure and Zogby Poll, "9/11+5 Reveals Dramatic Partisan Split," September 5, 2006, http://www.zogby.com/News/ReadNews.dbm?ID=1169.

52. Paul Wolfowitz, "Iraq, What Does Disarmament Look Like?," speech delivered at Council on Foreign Relations, January 23, 2003.

53. White House, "Interview of the Vice President by Tim Russert, NBC News, Meet the Press," September 10, 2006, http://www.whitehouse.gov/news/releases/2006/09/20060910.html.

54. White House, "President Discusses Foreign Policy During Visit to State Department," August 14, 2006, http://www.whitehouse.gov/news/releases/2006/08/2006/08/20060814-3.html.

55. Newt Gingrich, "The Third World War Has Begun," *Guardian*, July 20, 2006; interview, *Meet the Press*, NBC, July 16, 2006, http://www.msnbc.com; and "The Only Option Is to Win," *Washington Post*, August 11, 2006; and Rick Santorum, "The Great Test of This Generation," speech delivered at the National

Press Club, July 20, 2006, available at: http://www.national review.com.

56. Hassan M. Fattah, "Militia Rebuked by Some Arab Countries," *New York Times*, July 17, 2006.

57. Michel Bôle-Richard, "Le Fatah de Mahmoud Abbas défie le Hamas," *Le Monde*, January 8, 2007.

58. White House, "President Bush Delivers State of the Union Address," January 23, 2007, http://www.whitehouse.gov/news/releases/2007/01/20070123-2.html.

59. Glenn Kessler, "President's Portrayal of 'The Enemy' Flawed," *Washington Post*, January 24, 2007.

60. George W. Bush, "President Holds Primetime News Conference," Washington, D.C., October 11, 2001, quoted in Ivo H. Daalder and James M. Lindsay, *America Unbound: The Bush Revolution in Foreign Policy* (Washington, D.C.: Brookings Institution Press, 2003), 194. Two years later, in a television interview, Bush spoke of his intention to remind French president Jacques Chirac that "America is a good nation, genuinely good," in the hope that Chirac would come to understand the decisions he had made on Iraq. See the interview with Fox News's Brit Hume, "Text of Bush Interview," September 22, 2003, http://www.foxnews.com/story/0,2933,98006,00.html.

61. For the argument that "to be effective, multilateralism must be preceded by unilateralism," see Robert Kagan, "The Benevolent Empire," *Foreign Policy* (Summer 1998), 33. For other, similar arguments and a discussion of Bush's assertive leadership style, see Philip H. Gordon and Jeremy Shapiro, *Allies at War: America, Europe and the Crisis Over Iraq* (New York: McGraw-Hill, 2004), 49–55.

62. Bob Woodward, *Bush at War* (New York: Simon & Schuster, 2002), 81.

63. Bush quoted in Dan Balz, "President Puts Onus Back on Iraqi Leader," *Washington Post*, March 7, 2003. In the State of the Union Address in January of the following year, Bush's formulation was that "America will never seek a permission slip to defend the security of our country." See White House, "State of the Union Address," January 20, 2004.

64. Pew Global Attitudes Project, "America's Image Slips, But Allies Share U.S. Concerns Over Iran, Hamas," 15 Nation Survey, June

13, 2006, available at: http://pewglobal.org/reports/pdf/252.pdf. See similar results in German Marshall Fund of the United States, *Transatlantic Trends: Key Findings 2006* (Washington, D.C.: German Marshall Fund, 2006).

65. Pew Global Attitudes Project, "U.S. Image Up Slightly, But Still Negative," July 23, 2005, available at: http://pewglobal.org/reports/display.php?ReportID=247.

66. The average percentages of those with a "mainly negative" view were 52 percent in 2007, 47 percent in 2006, and 46 percent in 2005. The poll was conducted between November 2006 and January 2007 among 18,000 adults in eighteen countries by GlobeScan together with the Program on International Policy Attitudes (PIPA) at the University of Maryland. See http://www.worldpublicopinion.org/pipa/articles/home_page/306.php?nid=&id=&pnt=306&lb=hmpg1 (accessed January 23, 2007).

67. University of Maryland and Zogby International 2006 Annual Arab Public Opinion Survey, data available at: http://www.brookings.edu/views/speeches/telhami20070208.pdf. See also Shibley Tehami, *Reflections of Hearts and Minds: Media, Opinion, and Identity in the Arab World* (Washington, D.C.: Brookings Institution Press, forthcoming).

68. Max Boot, "Power: Resentment Comes with the Territory," *Washington Post*, March 3, 2003.

69. Kristol quoted in Maureen Dowd, "Hypocrisy and Apple Pie," *New York Times*, April 30, 2003. Also see Bill Kristol, *Fox News Sunday*, Fox News Network, April 27, 2003.

70. George W. Bush, "Address to a Joint Session of Congress and the American People," September 20, 2001; http://www.whitehouse.gov/news/releases/2001/09/20010920-8.html.

71. For Bush's reference to "Islamic fascists," see White House, "President Bush Discusses Terror Plot Upon Arrival in Wisconsin," August 10, 2006; http://www.whitehouse.gov/news/releases/2006/08/20060810-3.html. For Rumsfeld's evocations of Churchill, fascism, Nazism, and appeasement, see Donald H. Rumsfeld, "Address at the 88th Annual American Legion National Convention," Salt Lake City, Utah, August 29, 2006; http://www.defenselink.mil/Speeches/Speech.aspx?SpeechID=1033.

Cheney makes a parallel to Franklin Roosevelt and the "dirty business" of fighting wars in "Vice President's Remarks at Veterans of Foreign Wars National Convention," Reno, Nevada, August 28, 2006; http://www.whitehouse.gov/news/releases/2006/08/20060828-4.html.

72. Rumsfeld, "Address at the 88th Annual American Legion National Convention."

2. HOW WE WON THE COLD WAR

1. Harry S. Truman, "Address to a Joint Session of Congress, March 12, 1947"; http://yale.edu/lawweb/avalon/trudoc.htm.

2. Winston S. Churchill, "The Sinews of Peace," speech delivered at Westminster College, Fulton, Missouri, March 5, 1946: http://www.nato.int/docu/speech/1946/s460305a_e.htm.

3. See Time, June 20, 1949, quoted in Martin Walker, The Cold War: A History (New York: Henry Holt, 1993), 66–67.

4. John Lewis Gaddis, The Cold War: A New History (New York: Penguin Press, 2005), 39.

5. The full Khrushchev quotation is: "Whether you like it or not, history is on our side. We will bury you." According to Strobe Talbott, who translated Khrushchev's memoirs, what the Soviet leader meant was that the Soviet Union would outlast the West. See "We Will Bury You," Time, November 26, 1956, available at: http://www.time.com/time/magazine/article/0,9171,867329,00.htm; and discussion with Strobe Talbott, February 2007.

6. Walker, Cold War, 105.

7. George Kennan, "Telegraphic Message from Moscow," February 22, 1946, excerpts repr. in George F. Kennan, Memoirs: 1925–1950 (Boston: Little, Brown, 1967), 547–59, and X [pseud.], "The Sources of Soviet Conduct," Foreign Affairs (July 1947).

8. John Lewis Gaddis, Strategies of Containment: A Critical Appraisal of American National Security Policy During the Cold War, rev. ed. (Oxford, U.K.: Oxford University Press, 2005), 386.

9. Ron Suskind, The One Percent Doctrine: Deep Inside America's Pursuit of Its Enemies Since 9/11 (New York: Simon & Schuster, 2006).

10. General Leslie Groves on January 21, 1946, quoted in Marc Trachtenberg, "A 'Wasting Asset': American Strategy and the

Shifting Nuclear Balance, 1949–1954," *International Security* 13/3 (Winter 1988–89): 5.

11. Advocates of preventive war included the conservative writer James Burnham, the journalist William Laurence, U.S. Air Force Generals Curtis Le May and Orvil Anderson, nuclear scientist Leo Szilard, U.S. Navy Secretary Francis Matthews, and Senators Brien McMahon and John McClellan. Outside the United States, Winston Churchill was the most forceful advocate of "bringing matters to a head" while the United States still had an atomic monopoly. For details on the preventive war debate, see Trachtenberg, "A 'Wasting Asset'"; and Russell D. Buhite and William Christopher Hamel, "War for Peace: The Question of an American Preventive War Against the Soviet Union, 1945–1955," *Diplomatic History* 14 (Summer 1990): 367–84. Also see James Burnham, *The Struggle for the World* (New York: John Day Company, 1947).

12. Eisenhower quote from a March 25, 1954, NSC meeting, quoted in Trachtenberg, "A 'Wasting Asset,'" 40.

13. General Douglas MacArthur, "Farewell Address to Congress," April 19, 1951; available at: http://www.americanrhetoric.com/speeches/douglasmacarthurfarewelladdress.htm.

14. American Presidency Project, "Republican Party Platform of 1951," full text available at: http://www.presidency.ucsb.edu.

15. John Foster Dulles, "A Policy of Boldness," *Life*, May 19, 1952, 146–60.

16. Barry Goldwater, *The Conscience of a Conservative* (New York: Hillman Books, 1960), 96–97.

17. Dana H. Allin, *Cold War Illusions: America, Europe, and Soviet Power, 1969–1989* (New York: St. Martin's Press, 1994), 11.

18. Gaddis, *Strategies of Containment*, 386–87.

19. Kennan, "Telegraphic Message from Moscow."

20. Harold D. Lasswell, "The Garrison State," *American Journal of Sociology* (January 1941): 455–68. Also see Aaron L. Friedberg, "Why Didn't the United States Become a Garrison State?" *International Security* (Spring 1992); and *In the Shadow of the Garrison State* (Princeton, N.J.: Princeton University Press, 2000).

21. Hanson Baldwin, *The Price of Power* (New York: Harper, 1947), 18–20, quoted in Friedberg, "Garrison State," 111–12.

22. For a useful chart on U.S. defense spending (aggregates and as share of total federal spending and the GDP) from 1945 to 1992, see Gaddis, *Strategies of Containment*, 393–94. Original source: U.S. Office of Management and Budget, *The Budget for Fiscal Year 2005. Historical Series* (Washington, D.C., 2004), 45–50. The term "imperial overstretch" was popularized in Paul Kennedy, *The Rise and Fall of the Great Powers: Economic Change and Military Conflict from 1500 to 2000* (New York: Random House, 1987).

23. Truman quoted in Mary L. Dudziak, "Desegregation as a Cold War Imperative," *Stanford Law Review* 41 (November 1, 1988), 112, as quoted in Peter Beinart, *The Good Fight: Why Liberals, and Only Liberals, Can Win the War on Terror and Make America Great Again* (New York: HarperCollins, 2006), 10.

24. National Security Council, NSC-68, April 14, 1950.

25. Kennan, "Telegraphic Message from Moscow."

26. Quoted in Gaddis, *Strategies of Containment*, 133.

27. Ibid., 389.

28. Dwight D. Eisenhower, "Farewell Radio and Television Address to the American People," January 17, 1961, Dwight D. Eisenhower Library, http://www.eisenhower.archives.gov/farewell.htm.

29. From a Reagan radio address of May 1975, quoted in Kiron K. Skinner, Annelise Anderson, and Marin Anderson, eds., *Reagan, in His Own Hand* (New York: Free Press, 2001), 12.

30. From a Reagan radio address of May 25, 1977, quoted in Skinner, *Reagan, in His Own Hand*, 147.

31. From Reagan's first National Security Directive, "U.S. National Security Strategy," NSDD 32, May 20, 1982; quoted in Gaddis, *Strategies of Containment*, 355.

32. Reagan address to members of Parliament, London, June 8, 1982, *Public Papers of the Presidents: 1982* (Washington, D.C., 1983), 744–47; quoted in Gaddis, *Strategies of Containment*, 355–56.

33. "Excerpts from President's Speech to National Association of Evangelicals," *New York Times*, March 9, 1983.

34. Quoted in Gaddis, *Strategies of Containment*, 362.

35. Geir Lundestad, "Empire by Invitation? The United States and Western Europe, 1945–1952," *Journal of Peace Research* 23 (September 1986): 263–77.

36. Quoted in G. John Ikenberry, "Liberalism and Empire: Logics of Order in the American Unipolar Age," *Review of International Studies* (2004): 610.

37. Ibid., 610. For a good discussion of how countries that win wars can seek order through "strategic restraint," see G. John Ikenberry, *After Victory: Institutions, Strategic Restraint, and the Rebuilding of Order After Major Wars* (Princeton, N.J.: Princeton University Press, 2001).

38. Gaddis, *We Now Know: Rethinking Cold War History* (Oxford, U.K.: Clarendon Press, 1997), 201.

39. Reinhold Niebuhr, *The Irony of American History* (New York: Charles Scribner's Sons, 1952), 69, 138–39.

40. Harry S. Truman, "Special Message to the Congress on Civil Rights," February 2, 1948, *Public Papers of the Presidents of the United States*, January 1 to December 31, 1948 (Washington, D.C.: U.S. Government Printing Office, 1964), n. 20.

41. Gaddis, *Strategies of Containment*, 128.

42. Ibid., 128.

43. Eisenhower telephone conversation with Senator Styles Bridges, May 21, 1957, quoted in ibid., 152.

44. Johnson quoted in Richard Barnet, *The Alliance: America, Europe, Japan, Makers of the Postwar World* (New York: Simon & Schuster, 1983), 248. Also see Thomas Alan Schwartz, *Lyndon Johnson and Europe: In the Shadow of Vietnam* (Cambridge, Mass.: Harvard University Press, 2003).

45. Kissinger quoted in Frank Costigliola, *France and the United States: The Cold Alliance Since World War II* (New York: Twayne Publishers, 1992), 112–15.

46. Lawrence S. Kaplan, *NATO and the United States: The Enduring Alliance* (New York: Twayne Publishers, 1988), 181–82.

47. George F. Kennan, *American Diplomacy*, exp. ed. (Chicago: University of Chicago Press, 1984), 164.

48. George Kennan, Joint Orientation Conference, lecture, November 8, 1948, quoted in Gaddis, *Strategies of Containment*, 46.

49. Quoted in ibid., 46.

50. Rienhold Niebuhr in the *Chicago Sun Times*, November 11, 1948, quoted in Anatol Lieven and John Hulsman, *Ethical Realism: A*

Vision for America's Role in the World (New York: Pantheon, 2006), 42.

51. U.S. Department of State, "United States Policy Toward China," PPS/39, September 7, 1948, *Foreign Relations of the United States: 1948* (Washington, D.C.: U.S. Department of State, 1970–2003), vol. 8, 148; quoted in Gaddis, *Cold War*, 37.

52. Adams memo, March 8, 1949, quoted in Marc Jay Selverstone, "'All Roads Lead to Moscow': The United States, Great Britain, and the Communist Monolith," Ph.D. diss., Ohio University, 2000.

53. Harold P. Ford, "Calling the Sino-Soviet Split," http://www.cia.gov/csi/kent_csi/pdf/v42i5a05p.pdf; and Selverstone, "All Roads Lead to Moscow." Ford is quoted in Fareed Zakaria, "Mao & Stalin, Osama & Saddam," *Newsweek*, September 18, 2006.

54. Gaddis, *Strategies of Containment*, 139.

55. John Foster Dulles, speech delivered at Colgate University, July 7, 1950, quoted in John Lewis Gaddis, *The United States and the End of the Cold War: Implications, Reconsiderations, Provocations* (New York: Oxford University Press, 1992), 74.

56. All quoted in Gaddis, *Strategies of Containment*, 139.

57. Zakaria, "Mao & Stalin, Osama & Saddam."

3. THE RIGHT WAR

1. Glenn Kessler, "Rice Bucks Tradition with Pre-Election Appearances," *Washington Post*, November 4, 2006.

2. Robert Kagan, "Staying the Course, Win or Lose," *Washington Post*, November 2, 2006.

3. See Robert Kagan, *Of Paradise and Power: America and Europe in the New World Order* (New York: Knopf, 2003); and *Dangerous Nation: America's Place in the World from Its Earliest Days to the Dawn of the Twentieth Century* (New York: Knopf, 2006).

4. Colin Powell to John McCain, letter, September 13, 2006; available at: http://www.washingtonpost.com/wp-dyn/content/graphic/2006/09/14/GR2006091400728.html.

5. John Yoo, *War by Other Means: An Insider's Account of the War on Terror* (New York: Atlantic Monthly Press, 2006), 45.

6. U.S. Army, *Counterinsurgency*, par. 1–132, 6–10, 6–63.

7. David Galula, *Counterinsurgency Warfare: Theory and Practice* (St. Petersburg, Fla.: Hailer Publishing, 2005), 51 (orig. pub. 1964, Greenwood Press).

8. "A Place in the Sun, Beyond the Law," *The Economist*, May 8, 2003.

9. Galula, *Counterinsurgency Warfare*, 51–53; and James Hailer, "Detainees, If Freed, Could Help U.S.," *Washington Post*, July 24, 2006.

10. The 9/11 Commission stated: "The United States should engage its friends to develop a common coalition approach toward the detention and humane treatment of captured terrorists" and "New principles might draw upon Article 3 of the Geneva Conventions on the law of armed conflict." See *The 9/11 Commission Report: Final Report of the National Commission on Terrorist Attacks Upon the United States* (New York: W. W. Norton, 2004), 380.

11. Senator John McCain, "Statement on Detainee Amendments," Senate Floor Statement, October 5, 2005.

12. For Bush's claims, "President Discusses Creation of Military Commissions to Try Suspected Terrorists," September 6, 2006; http://www.whitehouse.gov/news/releases/2006/09/20060906 -3.html. For the CIA interrogator, Ron Suskind, *The One Percent Doctrine: Deep Inside the Pursuit of America's Enemies Since 9/11* (New York: Simon & Schuster, 2006), 100.

13. Intelligence Science Board, "Educing Information: Interrogation: Science and Art" (Washington, D.C.: Center for Strategic Intelligence Research, National Defense Intelligence College Press, December 2006); and Josh White, "Interrogation Research Is Lacking, Reports Says: Few Studies Have Examined U.S. Methods," *Washington Post*, January 16, 2007.

14. Lindsey Graham, "Rules for Our War," *Washington Post*, December 6, 2005.

15. The discussion is in Kurt M. Campbell and Michael E. O'Hanlon, *Hard Power: The New Politics of National Security* (New York: Basic Books, 2006), 122–26.

16. Ibid., 128.

17. Josh White and Ruben Castenada, "Laptop in Muhammad's Car Linked to Pr. George's Attack; Investigators Tie Sniper Suspects to Pizzeria Shootings," *Washington Post*, November 6, 2002.

18. Michael O'Hanlon and Jeremy Shapiro, "Introduction," in Michael d'Arcy, Michael O'Hanlon, Peter Orszag, Jeremy Shapiro, and James Steinberg, *Protecting the Homeland 2006/2007* (Washington, D.C.: Brookings Institution Press, 2006), 6.

19. For a detailed discussion of various proposals in these areas, ibid.; and Richard A. Falkenrath, "The 9/11 Commission Report: A Review Essay," *International Security* 29/3 (Winter 2004–2005): 170–90.

20. The projected Department of Homeland Security budget for 2007 was $42.7 billion; see http://www.dhs.gov/xabout/budget/. For the cost of tax cuts, see Greg Leiserson and Jeff Rohaly, "The Distribution of the 2001–2006 Tax Cuts," Tax Policy Center—A Joint Venture of the Urban Institute and Brookings Institution, November 15, 2006; available at: http://www.taxpolicycenter.org/UploadedPDF/411378_tax_cuts.pdf.

21. See Richard A. Posner, *Uncertain Shield: The U.S. Intelligence System in the Throes of Reform* (Lanham, Md.: Rowman & Littlefield, 2006), 87–117; and James Steinberg, "Intelligence Reform," in d'Arcy et al., *Protecting the Homeland 2006/2007*, 17–46, 47–72.

22. See "Arabic Speakers Still Scarce," *USA Today*, February 13, 2006; Dan Eggen, "FBI Agents Still Lacking Arabic Skills," *Washington Post*, October 11, 2006; and "Know Thine Enemy: Foreign Languages and Security," *The Economist*, May 7, 2005.

23. Peter Bergen, "Where've You Bin?," *The New Republic*, January 29, 2007.

24. Office of the Press Secretary, White House, "President Discusses Progress in the Global War on Terror," September 7, 2006, http://www.whitehouse.gov/news/releases/2006/09/20060907.html.

25. Kilcullen quoted in James Fallows, "Declaring Victory," *Atlantic Monthly*, September 2006.

26. John Mueller, *Overblown: How Politicians and the Terrorism Industry Inflate National Security Threats, and Why We Believe Them* (New York: Free Press, 2006), 13.

27. Brian Jenkins, *Unconquerable Nation: Knowing Our Enemy, Strengthening Ourselves* (Santa Monica, Calif.: RAND, 2006), 154–55.

28. See Helena K. Finn, "The Case for Cultural Diplomacy," *Foreign Affairs* (November–December 2003): 15–20.

29. For a good argument about the difference between democracy and constitutional liberalism, and why the United States should seek the latter before the former in the Middle East, see Fareed Zakaria, *The Future of Freedom: Illiberal Democracy at Home and Abroad* (New York: W. W. Norton, 2003).

30. For good discussions of these initiatives, see Tamara Cofman Wittes and Sarah E. Yerkes, *What Price Freedom? Assessing the Bush Administration's Freedom Agenda*, Analysis Paper Number 10 (Washington, D.C.: Saban Center for Middle East Policy, 2006); Madeleine K. Albright and Vin Weber, co-chairs, and Steven A. Cook, project director, *In Support of Arab Democracy: Why and How*, Council on Foreign Relations Independent Task Force Report No. 54 (2005); and Mary Jane Bolle, *Middle East Free Trade Area: Progress Report* (Washington, D.C.: Congressional Research Service, Library of Congress, updated July 3, 2006).

31. The Middle East Partnership Initiative saw its budget rise from $29 million in 2002 to $100 million in 2003, get cut by Congress and fall to $89.5 million in 2004 and $74.4 million in 2005, and rise back to $99 million in 2006. See Wittes and Yerkes, *What Price Freedom?*, 18.

32. Peter Bergen and Michael Lind, "A Matter of Pride," *Democracy: A Journal of Ideas* (Winter 2007), 8–16.

33. Susan E. Rice, "The Threat of Global Poverty," *National Interest* (Spring 2006): 76–82.

34. The classic assertion of this linkage is in Seymour Martin Lipset, "Some Social Requisites of Democracy: Economic Development and Political Legitimacy," *American Political Science Review* 53 (March 1959); see also Adam Przeworski and Fernando Limongi, "Modernization: Theories and Facts," *World Politics* 49/2 (January 1997); and the discussion in Zakaria, *The Future of Freedom*, 69–73.

35. See Edward Gresser, "Blank Spot on the Map: How Trade Policy Is Working Against the War on Terror," Progressive Policy Institute Report, February 2003, 1.

36. Intergovernmental Panel on Climate Change, "Climate Change 2007: A Physical Science Basis," February 2007; "President Bush

Delivers State of the Union Address," January 31, 2006, http://www.whitehouse.gov/stateoftheunion/2006/; and "President Bush Delivers State of the Union Address," January 23, 2007, http://www.whitehouse.gov/stateoftheunion/2007/.

37. See, for example, Michael L. Ross, "Does Oil Hinder Democracy?" *World Politics* 53 (2001): 325–61; and the discussion in "The Paradox of Plenty: The Curse of Oil," *The Economist*, December 24, 2005.

38. Thomas L. Friedman, "Big Talk, Little Will," *New York Times*, August 16, 2006.

39. Richard V. Allen, "The Man Who Changed the Game Plan," *National Interest* (Summer 1996): 96; see also Warm E. Norquist, "How the United States Used Competition to Win the Cold War," *Advances in Competitiveness Research* 10/1 (2002): 1–41.

40. Thomas L. Friedman, "The Oil-Addicted Ayatollah," *New York Times*, February 2, 2007.

41. David Sandalow, "Ending Oil Dependence," Brookings Institution, January 22, 2007; available at: http://www.brookings.edu/views/papers/fellows/sandalow20070122.pdf.

42. Calculations adapted from John Deutch and James R. Schlesinger, chairs, and David G. Victor, project director, *National Security Consequences of U.S. Oil Dependency*, Council on Foreign Relations Independent Task Force Report No. 58, 37.

43. Sandalow, "Ending Oil Dependence," 15.

44. "Americans Are Cautiously Open to Gas Tax Rise, Poll Shows," *New York Times*, February 28, 2006.

45. Wolfowitz was Deputy Secretary of Defense who went to the World Bank, Feith was Undersecretary of Defense for Policy who went to Georgetown University, and Bolton was Undersecretary of State who became U.S. Ambassador to the United Nations. Zoellick became Deputy Secretary of State, Zelikow became State Department Counselor, Burns became Undersecretary of State for Political Affairs, and Hill became Assistant Secretary of State for Asian Affairs and the administration's point person on North Korea.

46. George W. Bush, election debate with Al Gore, "Debate Transcript," October 11, 2000, available at: http://www.debates.org/pages/trans2000b.html.

4. A NEW DEAL FOR THE MIDDLE EAST

1. The flawed U.S. occupation of Iraq is well documented in Thomas Ricks, *Fiasco;* Michael R. Gordon and General Bernard E. Trainor, *Cobra II: The Inside Story of the Invasion and Occupation of Iraq* (New York: Pantheon, 2006); Bob Woodward, *State of Denial: Bush at War Part III* (New York: Simon & Schuster, 2006); and Rajiv Chandrasekaran, *Imperial Life in the Emerald City: Inside Iraq's Green Zone* (New York: Knopf, 2006).

2. For Cheney, see "Interview of the Vice President," by Jonathan Karl, USS *Kitty Hawk,* Yokosuka Naval Base, Japan, ABC News, February 21, 2007, http://www.whitehouse.gov/news/releases/2007/02/20070221.html.

3. ABC News/USA Today/BBC/ARD, "Iraq: Where Things Stand. Ebbing Hope in a Landscape of Loss Marks a National Survey of Iraq," March 19, 2007, http://abcnews.go.com/images/US/1033aIraqpoll.pdf. Also see the poll conducted in September 2006 for the Web site World Public Opinion by the Program on International Policy Attitudes (PIPA) at the University of Maryland, available at: http://www.worldpublicopinion.org/pipa/articles/brmiddleeastnafricara/250.php?nid=&id=&pnt=250&lb= (accessed February 27, 2007).

4. See, for example, Paul Wolfowitz's charge that by requiring the United States to deploy troops in Saudi Arabia, our containment policy gave Osama bin Laden "his principal talking point." "That was his big recruiting device, his big claim against us." Quoted in Ricks, *Fiasco,* 18.

5. "President Bush Discusses Care for America's Returning Wounded Warriors, War on Terror at American Legion," Renaissance Hotel, Washington, D.C., March 6, 2007, http://www.whitehouse.gov/news/releases/2007/03/20070306-1.html.

6. Joseph R. Biden Jr. and Leslie Gelb, "Unity Through Autonomy in Iraq," *New York Times,* May 1, 2006; and http://www.planforiraq.com.

7. Senate Committee on Foreign Relations, Hearings, *Supplemental Foreign Assistance Fiscal Year 1966—Vietnam* (Washington, D.C., 1966), 335–36, quoted in John Lewis Gaddis, *Strategies of Containment: A Critical Appraisal of American National Security*

Policy During the Cold War, rev. ed. (New York: Oxford University Press, 2005), 258.

8. Lawrence Wright, *The Looming Tower* (New York: Knopf, 2006), 38–39.

9. Ibid., 74.

10. Osama bin Laden, "Message to America," October 30, 2004, trans. in Bruce Lawrence, ed., *Messages to the World: The Statements of Osama bin Laden* (New York: Verso, 2005), 239.

11. Wright, *Looming Tower*, 307.

12. Reuters, Osama bin Laden Videotaped Statement, first broadcast October 7, 2001.

13. George Bush, "President Discusses the Future of Iraq," speech to the American Enterprise Institute, Washington Hilton Hotel, February 26, 2003.

14. For examples of the argument that "the road to Jerusalem will lead through Baghdad," see, among others, Henry A. Kissinger, "Iraq Is Becoming Bush's Most Difficult Challenge," *Chicago Tribune*, August 11, 2002; and Martin Peretz, "Son Shine; The New Bush Doctrine," *The New Republic*, September 9–16, 2002. Also see the discussion in "Birth of a Bush Doctrine?" *The Economist*, March 1, 2003; and Anatol Lieven, "A Mid-East Peace Cannot Be Fudged," *Financial Times*, September 11, 2003.

15. U.S. Dept. of State, Condoleezza Rice's "Press Availability with Palestinian Authority President Mahmoud Abbas," Ramallah, January 14, 2007, http://www.state.gov/secretary/rm/2007/78693 .htm; and David Makovsky, "Political Horizon: Enticing and Elusive," *International Herald Tribune*, February 13, 2007.

16. Philip Zelikow, "Building Security in the Broader Middle East," keynote address to the Weinberg Founders Conference 2006, Washington Institute for Near East Policy, September 15, 2006, transcript by Federal News Service, Washington, D.C.

17. Helene Cooper, "Philip Zelikow, Senior Aide to Rice, Resigns from Post," *New York Times*, November 28, 2006.

18. These basic elements are similar to those presented by President Clinton in what became known as the "Clinton Parameters" of December 23, 2000. The text of the Clinton Parameters is reprinted in Dennis Ross, *The Missing Peace: The Inside Story of the Fight*

for Middle East Peace (New York: Farrar, Straus and Giroux, 2004), 801–5.

19. "The Beirut Declaration on Saudi Peace Initiative," March 28, 2002, http://www.un.int/palestine/peace%20process/arabpi.html; and Karen DeYoung, "Saudi Prince Gave Bush 8-Point Mideast Peace Plan," *Washington Post,* April 27, 2002.

20. Joint Palestinian-Israeli Public Opinion Poll, PSR—Survey Research Unit, March 26, 2006, http://www.pcpsr.org/survey/polls/2006/p19ejoint.html.

21. Ephriam Yaar and Tamar Hermann, "Peace Index: December 2006," Tel Aviv University, http://www.spirit.tau.ac.il/xeddexcms008/download.asp?did=peaceindex2006_12_3-.

22. Shibley Telhami, University of Maryland/Zogby International 2006 Annual Arab Public Opinion Survey, available at: http://www.brookings.edu/views/speeches/telhami20070208.pdf.

23. International Crisis Group, *After Mecca: Engaging Hamas,* Middle East Report No. 62, February 28, 2007, 29–31.

24. Reuters, "Q & A Interview with Khaled Mashal," January 10, 2007; and "Khaled Meschaal: 'Il y aura un etat appelé Israël,'" *Le Monde,* January 12, 2007.

25. Fax provided to author by Trita Parsi of the National Iranian American Council. Also see Glenn Kessler, "In 2003, U.S. Spurned Iran's Offer of Dialogue; Some Officials Lament Lost Opportunity," *Washington Post,* June 18, 2006; and Glenn Kessler, "Rice Denies Seeing Iranian Proposal in '03," *Washington Post,* February 8, 2007.

26. With oil exports of around 2.5 million barrels per day, the increase in the oil price of over $30 per barrel between 2003 and 2006 brought Iran at least an extra $27 billion per year—for a total of around $47 billion in exports earnings in 2006.

27. See, for example, William Kristol, "And Now Iran," *Weekly Standard,* January 23, 2006; "It's Our War," *Weekly Standard,* July 24, 2006; Arthur Herman, "Getting Serious About Iran: A Military Option," *Commentary,* November 2006; Reuel Marc Gerecht, "To Bomb or Not to Bomb: That Is the Iran Question," *Weekly Standard,* April 24, 2006; and Michael Ledeen, "Delay," *National Review Online,* November 1, 2006.

28. Daniel L. Byman, "What Tehran Is Really Up To," *Washington Post*, February 18, 2007; Dafna Linzer, "Troops Authorized to Kill Iranian Operatives in Iraq; Administration Strategy Stirs Concern Among Some Officials," *Washington Post*, January 26, 2007.

29. The option of relying on Israel to strike Iranian targets, which has been invoked by Vice President Dick Cheney and others, would be even more counterproductive than an American attack. With twenty-five F-15I long-range strike fighters, the Israeli air force might have the capacity to strike key nuclear targets in Iran even without direct help from the United States. But given the distances involved (in some cases more than 1,000 miles), the fighters would have to carry so much fuel that their payloads would be limited and there would be no time for repeated strikes, meaning that Israel would inevitably conduct the operation even less effectively than the United States. Americans would bear all the consequences of the strikes anyway, as no one would believe that Israel would act without close coordination with Washington, not least because of the Israeli need to fly over U.S.-controlled airspace in Iraq on the way to Iran. Israel also has Jericho II missiles that could reach Iran, but not with adequate accuracy or payload, and it has around 350 F-16s, but they would need refueling over Iraqi and Jordanian airspace, which would be exceedingly difficult. See Kenneth M. Pollack, *The Persian Puzzle: The Conflict Between Iran and America* (New York: Random House, 2005), 391–95.

30. Iran has always insisted it has a right to uranium enrichment based on Article IV of the Nuclear Nonproliferation Treaty (NPT), which grants signatories the "inalienable right to develop research, production and use of nuclear energy for peaceful purposes." While there is a debate among legal experts about whether that phrase should be interpreted as including the right to the full nuclear fuel-cycle—many argue it does not—UNSCR 1696 makes that debate moot, since it demands that Iran "suspend all enrichment-related and reprocessing activities." The Security Council took the view—based on the IAEA's 2003 finding that Iran had been secretly operating a uranium enrichment program and importing illicit nuclear technology for eighteen years—that Iran had violated Article II of the NPT, which obliges signatories

"not to seek or receive assistance in the manufacture of nuclear weapons or other nuclear explosive devises," and that it could not invoke one Treaty Article to defend its actions while it was in violation of another. Article 10 of the UN Charter, moreover, clarifies that "in the event of a conflict between the obligations of the Members of the United Nations under the present Charter and their obligations under any other international agreement, their obligations under the present Charter shall prevail." UNSCR 1696, in other words, supersedes the NPT. See Amy Reed, "UN Resolution 1696 Moots Iranian Legal Claim," *Proliferation News*, Carnegie Endowment for International Peace, August 21, 2006, http://www.proliferationnews.org.

31. Thom Shanker, "Security Council Votes to Tighten Iran Sanctions," *New York Times*, March 25, 2007.

32. Jad Mouawad, "West Adds to Strains on Iran's Lifeline," *New York Times*, February 13, 2007; and Roger Stern, "The Iranian Petroleum Crisis and United States National Security," *Proceedings of the National Academy of Sciences of the United States of America*, published online December 26, 2006, available at: http://www.pnas.org.

33. Kim Murphy, "Dissent Grows in Iran," *Los Angeles Times*, February 8, 2007. Also see Nazila Fathi, "Iran President Facing Revival of Students' Ire," *New York Times*, December 21, 2006; and David Ignatius, "Signals from Tehran," *Washington Post*, February 23, 2007.

34. Associated Press, "Iranians Deal Blow to Ahmadinejad," *International Herald Tribune*, December 18, 2006.

35. Howard LaFranchi, "West's Iran Plan Shows Gains: Will US Stick to It?" *Christian Science Monitor*, January 23, 2007.

36. Associated Press, "Iran's Most Senior Dissident Cleric Criticizes Ahmadinejad Over Nuclear Diplomacy, Inflation," *International Herald Tribune*, January 22, 2007.

37. Mehdi Khalaji, "Iran Feels the Heat: International Pressure Emboldens Tehran's Domestic Critics," Washington Institute for Near East Policy, Policy Watch no. 1185, January 18, 2007.

38. The case for a grand bargain is made in Michael McFaul, Abbas Milani, and Larry Diamond, "A Win-Win U.S. Strategy for Dealing with Iran," *Washington Quarterly* (Winter 2006–7), 121–38.

39. Figures of the U.S. commander in Afghanistan, Lieutenant General Karl Eikenberry, quoted in James Dobbins, "Ending Afghanistan's Civil War," testimony presented before the House Armed Services Committee on January 30, 2007 (RAND CT-271, January 2007). Also see Karl F. Inderfurth and Bruce Riedel, "More, NATO, More," *International Herald Tribune,* February 6, 2007.

40. Carlotta Gall, "Record Opium Crop Possible in Afghanistan, U.N. Study Predicts," *New York Times,* March 6, 2007.

41. The poll was conducted by Charney Research for ABC News/BBC World Service in November 2006. Craig Charney and Gary Langer, "Misunderstanding Afghanistan," *Washington Post,* December 17, 2006.

42. James Dobbins, John G. McGinn, Keith Crane, Seth G. Jones, Rollie Lal, Andrew Rathmell, Rachel Swanger, and Anga Timilsina, *America's Role in Nation-Building: From Germany to Iraq* (Washington, D.C.: RAND, 2003), 157.

43. Dobbins, "Ending Afghanistan's Civil War."

44. Though there were 18.6 peacekeepers per thousand people in Bosnia and 20 per thousand in Kosovo, in Afghanistan from 2003 to 2007 there were on average less than two peacekeepers per thousand Afghans. See Dobbins et al., *America's Role in Nation-Building,* 36.

45. Barnett Rubin estimates that some 60,000 experienced fighters demobilized after the fall of the Taliban and have found "work" other than in the Afghan National Army. Barnett R. Rubin, "Saving Afghanistan," *Foreign Affairs* (January–February 2007).

46. Frederick Barton, Karin von Hippel, Seema Patel, and Steven Ross, *Breaking Point: Measuring Progress in Afghanistan* (Washington, D.C.: Center for Strategic and International Studies, February 23, 2007); and Haroun Mir, "Bolster the Afghan National Army," *International Herald Tribune,* February 17–18, 2007.

47. Mir, "Bolster the Afghan National Army."

48. Bruce Riedel, "Al Qaeda Strikes Back," *Foreign Affairs* (May–June 2007).

49. James Jones and Mansoor Ijaz, "Pakistan Holds the Key to South Asia's Security," *Financial Times,* February 22, 2007.

50. The United States also provides $5 billion in credit guarantees for the purchase of U.S.-made F-16 fighter planes and supports post-

ponement of payment of $13.5 billion in Pakistani debt. *U.S. Loans & Grants,* USAID, http://qesdb.usaid.gov/cgi-bin/broker.exe (accessed March 6, 2007). Also see Craig Cohen and Derek Chollet, "When $10 Billion Is Not Enough: Rethinking U.S. Strategy Toward Pakistan," *Washington Quarterly* (Spring 2007): 7–19; and Selig S. Harrison, "Pressuring Pakistan," *International Herald Tribune,* February 23, 2007.

51. Griff Witte and Kamran Khan, "Arrest in Pakistan Spurs Hope of Stronger Effort," *Washington Post,* March 3, 2007.

52. The figure for Turkey was less than for Pakistan, and 20 points less than in France. Pew Global Attitudes Survey, "America's Global Image Slips, But Allies Share U.S. Concern Over Iran, Hamas," June 13, 2006; available at: http://pewglobal.org/reports/pdf/252.pdf.

53. In a 2006 German Marshall Fund of the United States poll, Iran scored a 43 on a "thermometer" of Turkish feelings toward different countries while the United States scored just 20. The data on the United States as a threat to peace and security is from a January 2005 BBC World Service poll conducted in twenty-one countries. Karl Vick, "In Many Turks' Eyes, U.S. Remains the Enemy," *Washington Post,* April 10, 2005.

54. Ali Carkoglu and Kemal Kirisci, "The View from Turkey: Perceptions of Greeks and Greek-Turkish Rapprochement by the Turkish Mass Public," *Turkish Studies* 5/1 (Winter 2004).

5. WHAT VICTORY WILL LOOK LIKE

1. John Lewis Gaddis, "How the Cold War Might End," *The Atlantic Monthly,* November 5, 1987.

2. Gaddis grades his attempt at imagining the end of the Cold War in John Lewis Gaddis, *The United States and the End of the Cold War: Implications, Reconsiderations, Provocations* (New York: Oxford University Press, 1992), 154.

3. From Reagan's address to the members of the British Parliament, London, June 8, 1982, *Public Papers of the Presidents: 1982* (Washington, D.C.: General Services Administration, National Archives and Records Service, Office of the Federal Register, 1983), 744–47.

4. Ronald Reagan, *An American Life* (New York: Simon & Schuster), 683.

5. Richard Perle, "Memorandum; To: President Reagan, From: Richard Perle," *U.S. News & World Report,* December 14, 1987. For Scowcroft, who explained that he feared Gorbachev would "revitalize" the Soviet system to better "compete with the West," George Bush and Brent Scowcroft, *A World Transformed* (New York: Knopf, 1998), 13. Also see the discussion in Frances Fitzgerald, *Way Out There in the Blue: Reagan, Star Wars, and the End of the Cold War* (New York: Simon & Schuster, 2000), 473.

6. Director of National Intelligence, "Soviet Policy Toward the West: The Gorbachev Challenge," National Intelligence Estimate 11-4-89, April 1, 1989.

7. Everett Carll Ladd, "In US, a New View of the East in '89," *Christian Science Monitor,* December 26, 1989.

8. In a 2005 letter from Ayman al-Zawahiri to the Jordanian-born terrorist Abu Musab al-Zarqawi, the leader of al Qaeda in Iraq until his death in June 2006, al-Zawahiri outlines the stages of the al Qaeda plan as follows. First stage: Expel the Americans from Iraq. Second stage: Establish an Islamic authority or amirate, then develop it and support it until it achieves the level of a caliphate. Third stage: Extend the jihad wave to the secular countries neighboring Iraq. Fourth stage: Clash with Israel, because Israel was established only to challenge any new Islamic entity. See al-Zawahiri to al-Zarqawi, letter, July 9, 2005, available at: http://www.globalsecurity.org/security/library/report/2005/zawahiri zarqawi-letter_9jul2005.htm.

9. Louise Richardson, *What Terrorists Want* (New York: Random House, 2006), 232.

10. David Frum and Richard Perle, *An End to Evil: How to Win the War on Terror* (New York: Random House, 2003), 9.

11. For Jordan polls, Pew Global Attitudes Project, "The Great Divide: How Westerners and Muslims View Each Other," June 22, 2006, http://pewglobal.org/reports/display.php?ReportID=253. Also see Mueller, *Overblown,* 185.

12. Marc Lynch, "Al-Qaeda's Media Strategies," *National Interest* (Summer 2006); and Peter Bergen, interviewed by Aziz Huq, American Prospect Online, January 19, 2006, http://www.prospect.org/web/page.ww?section=root&name=ViewWeb&articleId=10855.

13. Ned Parker, "Insurgents Report a Split with Al-Qaeda in Iraq," *Los Angeles Times*, March 27, 2007; Sudarsan Raghavan, "Sunni Factions Split with Al-Qaeda Group," *Washington Post*, April 14, 2007; and Bing West and Owen West, "Iraq's Real 'Civil War,'" *Wall Street Journal*, April 5, 2007.

14. Quoted in Fallows, "Declaring Victory," *The Atlantic Monthly*, September 2006.

15. Peter Bergen, "Where You Bin?," *The New Republic*, January 29, 2007.

16. Marc Lynch, "Taking Arabs Seriously," *Foreign Affairs* (September–October 2003).

17. University of Maryland/Zogby International 2006 Annual Arab Public Opinion Survey, available at http://www.brookings.edu/views/speeches/telhami20070208.pdf.

18. For scholarly arguments that political Islam is already failing and likely to fail in the long run, see Olivier Roy, *The Failure of Political Islam* (Cambridge, Mass.: Harvard University Press, 1996); Roy, *Globalized Islam*; Gilles Kepel, *Jihad: The Trail of Political Islam* (Cambridge, Mass.: Harvard University Press, 2002); and Gilles Kepel, *The War for Muslim Minds: Islam and the West* (Cambridge, Mass.: Belknap Press, 2004).

19. Faiza Saleh Ambah, "New Clicks in the Arab World. Bloggers Challenge Longtime Cultural, Political Restrictions," *Washington Post*, November 12, 2006.

20. Lynch, "Taking Arabs Seriously."

★ ★ **★ Acknowledgments**

A number of colleagues and friends provided indispensable support for this project. They will not all agree with every word in the final product, but whatever misjudgments or mistakes I've made would have been greater without their input.

At Brookings, Strobe Talbott and Carlos Pascual gave me unwavering support and excellent guidance—even while writing books and managing countless projects of their own. Jeremy Shapiro, an expert on counterterrorism (among many other things) and sometime coauthor, read every chapter and as usual provided challenging, insightful, and constructive comments. Allison Hart was the best research assistant an author could ask for, providing her own considerable expertise on the Islamic world and helping to track down information on everything from cellulosic ethanol to George F. Kennan.

Paul Golob was a brilliant editor who helped sharpen my thesis, tightened my prose, and made sure I met his often unreasonable deadlines. I'm grateful to Gideon Rose, managing editor of *Foreign Affairs,* for putting me in touch with

Paul, encouraging me to write this book, and for publishing an article of mine ("The End of the Bush Revolution," *Foreign Affairs*, July–August 2006), which initially aired some of the ideas in this book. My agent, Rafe Sagalyn, generously shared his exhaustive knowledge of the publishing world and helped move the book from a mere idea to a (hopefully successful) finished product.

Other experts both at Brookings and elsewhere provided useful, critical comments on all or parts of my initial draft. I thank Dana Allin, Daniel Benjamin, Daniel Byman, James Dobbins, John Lewis Gaddis, Tom Malinowski, Andrew Moffat, James O'Brien, Michael O'Hanlon, Paul Pillar, Bruce Riedel, David Sandalow, Steven Simon, and Omer Taspinar for their contributions.

The Rockefeller Brothers Fund provided generous financial assistance for my research, and I thank its president, Stephen Heintz, for his support.

Finally, warmest thanks of all to my wife, Rachel, and my children, Noah, Ben, and Dinah. They give me a lot more than good comments.

★ ★ ★ Index

★ ★ ★ About the Author

Philip H. Gordon is senior fellow for U.S. foreign policy at the Brookings Institution. He previously served on the National Security Council staff and has taught at the Johns Hopkins University School of Advanced International Studies in Washington, D.C., and at INSEAD in France and Singapore. He is the author or coauthor of five books on international affairs and U.S. foreign policy, and his articles have appeared in *The New York Times, The Washington Post, Financial Times, The Wall Street Journal,* and *Foreign Affairs.* He lives in Washington, D.C., with his wife and three children.